OpenCV 3.x with Python By Example

Second Edition

Make the most of OpenCV and Python to build applications for object recognition and augmented reality

Gabriel Garrido
Prateek Joshi

BIRMINGHAM - MUMBAI

OpenCV 3.x with Python By Example
Second Edition

Commissioning Editor: Aaron Lazar
Acquisition Editor: Chaitanya Nair
Content Development Editor: Rohit Kumar Singh
Technical Editor: Ketan Kamble
Copy Editor: Safis Editing
Project Coordinator: Vaidehi Sawant
Proofreader: Safis Editing
Indexer: Rekha Nair
Graphics Coordinator: Jason Monteiro
Production Coordinator: Shraddha Falebhai

First published: September 2015
Second edition: January 2018

Production reference: 1150118

Published by Packt Publishing Ltd.
Livery Place
35 Livery Street
Birmingham
B3 2PB, UK.

ISBN 978-1-78839-690-5

www.packtpub.com

Contributors

About the authors

Gabriel Garrido is a multifaceted and versatile software engineer with more than 7 years of experience in developing web applications for companies such as Telefonica, Trivago, and Base7Booking. He has a degree in computer science from the University of Granada, Spain.

He is passionate about coding, focusing on its quality and spending hours working on personal projects based on technologies such as computer vision, artificial intelligence, and augmented reality. Taking part in hackathons is one of his hobbies. He has won a couple of prizes for implementing beta software for a Google Cardboard hackathon and another for a travel assistant at a TNOOZ hackathon.

I'd like to thank each one of the colleagues that I've had close to me throughout all these years working in the software industry for helping me enhance my knowledge and my experience in this amazing world of hacking.

Prateek Joshi is an artificial intelligence researcher, an author of eight published books, and a TEDx speaker. He has been featured in Forbes 30 Under 30, CNBC, TechCrunch, Silicon Valley Business Journal, and many more publications. He is the founder of Pluto AI, a venture-funded Silicon Valley start-up building an intelligence platform for water facilities. He has been an invited speaker at technology and entrepreneurship conferences including TEDx, Global Big Data Conference, Machine Learning Developers Conference, Sensors Expo, and more. His tech blog has more than 1.6 million page views from over 200 countries, and he has more than 7,400 followers. He graduated from the University of Southern California with a master's degree specializing in Artificial Intelligence. He has previously worked at NVIDIA and Microsoft Research. You can learn more about him on his personal website.

About the reviewer

Naren Yellavula, better known as Naren Arya in the developer community, is a Python and Go developer from Bangalore, India. He works as software engineer level two for Citrix R&D India, and as a full stack developer, he develops single-page applications and microservices. He loves the UNIX philosophy and blogs about programming. He has also been a speaker at various developer conferences, such as PyCon India 2015 and 2017. When he's not staring at his computer screen, he enjoys reading books.

> *I really appreciate Prateek and Gabriel for their passion in writing this amazing book. This book covers a wide range of topics on computer vision and AI. As an initial reader in the reviewing process, I enjoyed reading this book thoroughly. I also sincerely congratulate the editorial team for their hard work in polishing and iterating the book. All the best!*

Packt is searching for authors like you

If you're interested in becoming an author for Packt, please visit `authors.packtpub.com` and apply today. We have worked with thousands of developers and tech professionals, just like you, to help them share their insight with the global tech community. You can make a general application, apply for a specific hot topic that we are recruiting an author for, or submit your own idea.

`mapt.io`

Mapt is an online digital library that gives you full access to over 5,000 books and videos, as well as industry leading tools to help you plan your personal development and advance your career. For more information, please visit our website.

Why subscribe?

- Spend less time learning and more time coding with practical eBooks and Videos from over 4,000 industry professionals

- Improve your learning with Skill Plans built especially for you

- Get a free eBook or video every month

- Mapt is fully searchable

- Copy and paste, print, and bookmark content

PacktPub.com

Did you know that Packt offers eBook versions of every book published, with PDF and ePub files available? You can upgrade to the eBook version at `www.PacktPub.com` and as a print book customer, you are entitled to a discount on the eBook copy. Get in touch with us at `service@packtpub.com` for more details.

At `www.PacktPub.com`, you can also read a collection of free technical articles, sign up for a range of free newsletters, and receive exclusive discounts and offers on Packt books and eBooks.

Table of Contents

Preface

Computer vision is found everywhere in modern technology. OpenCV for Python enables us to run computer vision algorithms in real time. With the advent of powerful machines, we are getting more processing power to work with. Using this technology, we can seamlessly integrate our computer vision applications into the cloud. Web developers can develop complex applications without having to reinvent the wheel. This book is a practical tutorial that covers various examples at different levels, teaching you about the different functions of OpenCV and their actual implementations.

Who this book is for

This book is intended for Python developers who are new to OpenCV and want to develop computer vision applications with OpenCV and Python. This book is also useful for generic software developers who want to deploy computer vision applications on the cloud. It would be helpful to have some familiarity with basic mathematical concepts such as vectors and matrices.

What this book covers

Chapter 1, *Applying Geometric Transformations to Images*, explains how to apply geometric transformations to images. In this chapter, we will discuss affine and projective transformations and see how we can use them to apply cool geometric effects to photos. The chapter will begin with the procedure of installing OpenCV-Python on multiple platforms, such as Mac OS X, Linux, and Windows. You will also learn how to manipulate an image in various ways, such as resizing and changing color spaces.

Chapter 2, *Detecting Edges and Applying Image Filters*, shows how to use fundamental image-processing operators and how we can use them to build bigger projects. We will discuss why we need edge detection and how it can be used in various different ways in computer vision applications. We will discuss image filtering and how we can use it to apply various visual effects to photos.

Chapter 3, *Cartoonizing an Image*, shows how to cartoonize a given image using image filters and other transformations. We will see how to use the webcam to capture a live video stream. We will discuss how to build a real-time application, where we extract information from each frame in the stream and display the result.

Chapter 4, *Detecting and Tracking Different Body Parts*, shows how to detect and track faces in a live video stream. We will discuss the face detection pipeline and see how we can use it to detect and track different parts of the face, such as eyes, ears, mouth, and nose.

Chapter 5, *Extracting Features from an Image*, is about detecting the salient points (called keypoints) in an image. We will discuss why these salient points are important and how we can use them to understand the image's content. We will talk about the different techniques that can be used to detect salient points and extract features from an image.

Chapter 6, *Seam Carving*, shows how to do content-aware image resizing. We will discuss how to detect interesting parts of an image and see how we can resize a given image without deteriorating those interesting parts.

Chapter 8, *Detecting Shapes and Segmenting an Image*, shows how to perform image segmentation. We will discuss how to partition a given image into its constituent parts in the best possible way. You will also learn how to separate the foreground from the background in an image.

Chapter 8, *Object Tracking*, shows you how to track different objects in a live video stream. At the end of this chapter, you will be able to track any object in a live video stream that is captured through the webcam.

Chapter 9, *Object Recognition*, shows how to build an object recognition system. We will discuss how to use this knowledge to build a visual search engine.

Chapter 10, *Augmented Reality*, shows how to build an augmented reality application. By the end of this chapter, you will be able to build a fun augmented reality project using the webcam.

Chapter 11, *Machine Learning by Artificial Neural Network*, shows how to build advanced image classifiers and object recognition using the latest OpenCV implementations. By the end of this chapter, you will be able to understand how neural networks work and how to apply them to machine learning to build advance images tools.

To get the most out of this book

You'll need the following software:

- OpenCV 3.1 or higher
- NumPy 1.13 or higher
- SciPy 1.0 or higher
- scikit-learn 0.19 or higher
- pickleshare 0.7 or higher

The hardware specifications requirement is any computer with at least 8 GB DDR3 RAM.

Download the example code files

You can download the example code files for this book from your account at `www.packtpub.com`. If you purchased this book elsewhere, you can visit `www.packtpub.com/support` and register to have the files emailed directly to you.

You can download the code files by following these steps:

1. Log in or register at `www.packtpub.com`.
2. Select the **SUPPORT** tab.
3. Click on **Code Downloads & Errata**.
4. Enter the name of the book in the **Search** box and follow the onscreen instructions.

Once the file is downloaded, please make sure that you unzip or extract the folder using the latest version of:

- WinRAR/7-Zip for Windows
- Zipeg/iZip/UnRarX for Mac
- 7-Zip/PeaZip for Linux

The code bundle for the book is also hosted on GitHub at `https://github.com/PacktPublishing/OpenCV-3-x-with-Python-By-Example`. We also have other code bundles from our rich catalog of books and videos available at `https://github.com/PacktPublishing/`. Check them out!

Download the color images

We also provide a PDF file that has color images of the screenshots/diagrams used in this book. You can download it here:
`http://www.packtpub.com/sites/default/files/downloads/OpenCV3xwithPythonByExample_ColorImages.pdf`.

Conventions used

There are a number of text conventions used throughout this book.

`CodeInText`: Indicates code words in text, database table names, folder names, filenames, file extensions, pathnames, dummy URLs, user input, and Twitter handles. Here is an example: "The `imwrite()` method will save the grayscale image as an output file named `output.png`."

A block of code is set as follows:

```
import cv2
img = cv2.imread('images/input.jpg')
cv2.imwrite('images/output.png', img, [cv2.IMWRITE_PNG_COMPRESSION])
```

When we wish to draw your attention to a particular part of a code block, the relevant lines or items are set in bold:

```
import cv2
img = cv2.imread('images/input.jpg')
cv2.imwrite('images/output.png', img, [cv2.IMWRITE_PNG_COMPRESSION])
```

Any command-line input or output is written as follows:

```
$ pip install numpy
```

Bold: Indicates a new term, an important word, or words that you see onscreen. For example, words in menus or dialog boxes appear in the text like this. Here is an example: "**RGB**: Probably the most popular color space. It stands for Red, Green, and Blue."

 Warnings or important notes appear like this.

Tips and tricks appear like this.

Get in touch

Feedback from our readers is always welcome.

General feedback: Email `feedback@packtpub.com` and mention the book title in the subject of your message. If you have questions about any aspect of this book, please email us at `questions@packtpub.com`.

Errata: Although we have taken every care to ensure the accuracy of our content, mistakes do happen. If you have found a mistake in this book, we would be grateful if you would report this to us. Please visit `www.packtpub.com/submit-errata`, selecting your book, clicking on the Errata Submission Form link, and entering the details.

Piracy: If you come across any illegal copies of our works in any form on the Internet, we would be grateful if you would provide us with the location address or website name. Please contact us at `copyright@packtpub.com` with a link to the material.

If you are interested in becoming an author: If there is a topic that you have expertise in and you are interested in either writing or contributing to a book, please visit `authors.packtpub.com`.

Reviews

Please leave a review. Once you have read and used this book, why not leave a review on the site that you purchased it from? Potential readers can then see and use your unbiased opinion to make purchase decisions, we at Packt can understand what you think about our products, and our authors can see your feedback on their book. Thank you!

For more information about Packt, please visit `packtpub.com`.

1
Applying Geometric Transformations to Images

In this chapter, we are going to learn how to apply cool geometric effects to images. Before we get started, we need to install OpenCV-Python. We will explain how to compile and install the necessary libraries to follow every example in this book.

By the end of this chapter, you will know:

- How to install OpenCV-Python
- How to read, display, and save images
- How to convert to multiple color spaces
- How to apply geometric transformations such as translation, rotation, and scaling
- How to use affine and projective transformations to apply funny geometric effects to photos

Installing OpenCV-Python

In this section, we explain how to install OpenCV 3.X with Python 2.7 on multiple platforms. If you desire it, OpenCV 3.X also supports the use of Python 3.X and it will be fully compatible with the examples in this book. Linux is recommended as the examples in this book were tested on that OS.

Windows

In order to get OpenCV-Python up and running, we need to perform the following steps:

1. **Install Python**: Make sure you have Python 2.7.x installed on your machine. If you don't have it, you can install it from: `https://www.python.org/downloads/windows/`.

2. **Install NumPy**: NumPy is a great package to do numerical computing in Python. It is very powerful and has a wide variety of functions. OpenCV-Python plays nicely with NumPy, and we will be using this package a lot during the course of this book. You can install the latest version from: `http://sourceforge.net/projects/numpy/files/NumPy/`.

We need to install all these packages in their default locations. Once we install Python and NumPy, we need to ensure that they're working fine. Open up the Python shell and type the following:

```
>>> import numpy
```

If the installation has gone well, this shouldn't throw up any errors. Once you confirm it, you can go ahead and download the latest OpenCV version from: `http://opencv.org/downloads.html`.

Once you finish downloading it, double-click to install it. We need to make a couple of changes, as follows:

1. Navigate to `opencv/build/python/2.7/`.
2. You will see a file named `cv2.pyd`. Copy this file to `C:/Python27/lib/site-packages`.

You're all set! Let's make sure that OpenCV is working. Open up the Python shell and type the following:

```
>>> import cv2
```

If you don't see any errors, then you are good to go! You are now ready to use OpenCV-Python.

macOS X

To install OpenCV-Python, we will be using Homebrew. Homebrew is a great package manager for macOS X and it will come in handy when you are installing various libraries and utilities on macOS X. If you don't have Homebrew, you can install it by running the following command in your terminal:

```
$ ruby -e "$(curl -fsSL
https://raw.githubusercontent.com/Homebrew/install/master/install)"
```

Even though OS X comes with inbuilt Python, we need to install Python using Homebrew to make our lives easier. This version is called brewed Python. Once you install Homebrew, the next step is to install brewed Python. Open up the terminal, and type the following:

```
$ brew install python
```

This will automatically install it as well. Pip is a package management tool to install packages in Python, and we will be using it to install other packages. Let's make sure the brewed Python is working correctly. Go to your terminal and type the following:

```
$ which python
```

You should see /usr/local/bin/python printed on the terminal. This means that we are using the brewed Python, and not the inbuilt system Python. Now that we have installed brewed Python, we can go ahead and add the repository, homebrew/science, which is where OpenCV is located. Open the terminal and run the following command:

```
$ brew tap homebrew/science
```

Make sure the NumPy package is installed. If not, run the following in your terminal:

```
$ pip install numpy
```

Now, we are ready to install OpenCV. Go ahead and run the following command from your terminal:

```
$ brew install opencv --with-tbb --with-opengl
```

OpenCV is now installed on your machine, and you can find it at `/usr/local/Cellar/opencv/3.1.0/`. You can't use it just yet. We need to tell Python where to find our OpenCV packages. Let's go ahead and do that by symlinking the OpenCV files. Run the following commands from your terminal (please, double check that you are actually using the right versions, as they might be slightly different):

```
$ cd /Library/Python/2.7/site-packages/
$ ln -s /usr/local/Cellar/opencv/3.1.0/lib/python2.7/site-packages/cv.py
cv.py
$ ln -s /usr/local/Cellar/opencv/3.1.0/lib/python2.7/site-packages/cv2.so
cv2.so
```

You're all set! Let's see if it's installed properly. Open up the Python shell and type the following:

```
> import cv2
```

If the installation went well, you will not see any error messages. You are now ready to use OpenCV in Python.

If you want to use OpenCV within a virtual environment, you could follow the instructions in the *Virtual environments* section, applying small changes to each of the commands for macOS X.

Linux (for Ubuntu)

First, we need to install the OS requirements:

```
[compiler] $ sudo apt-get install build-essential
[required] $ sudo apt-get install cmake git libgtk2.0-dev pkg-config
           libavcodec-dev libavformat-dev libswscale-dev git
           libgstreamer0.10-dev libv4l-dev
[optional] $ sudo apt-get install python-dev python-numpy libtbb2
           libtbb-dev libjpeg-dev libpng-dev libtiff-dev libjasper-dev
           libdc1394-22-dev
```

Once the OS requirements are installed, we need to download and compile the latest version of OpenCV along with several supported flags to let us implement the following code samples. Here we are going to install Version 3.3.0:

```
$ mkdir ~/opencv
$ git clone -b 3.3.0 https://github.com/opencv/opencv.git opencv
$ cd opencv
$ git clone https://github.com/opencv/opencv_contrib.git opencv_contrib
```

```
$ mkdir release
$ cd release
$ cmake -D CMAKE_BUILD_TYPE=RELEASE -D CMAKE_INSTALL_PREFIX=/usr/local  -D
INSTALL_PYTHON_EXAMPLES=ON   -D INSTALL_C_EXAMPLES=OFF -D
OPENCV_EXTRA_MODULES_PATH=~/opencv/opencv_contrib/modules -D
BUILD_PYTHON_SUPPORT=ON -D WITH_XINE=ON -D WITH_OPENGL=ON -D WITH_TBB=ON -D
WITH_EIGEN=ON -D BUILD_EXAMPLES=ON -D BUILD_NEW_PYTHON_SUPPORT=ON -D
WITH_V4L=ON -D BUILD_EXAMPLES=ON ../
$ make -j4 ; echo 'Running in 4 jobs'
$ sudo make install
```

If you are using Python 3, place -D + flags together, as you see in the following command:

```
cmake -DCMAKE_BUILD_TYPE=RELEASE....
```

Virtual environments

If you are using virtual environments to keep your test environment completely separate from the rest of your OS, you could install a tool called **virtualenvwrapper** by following this tutorial: https://virtualenvwrapper.readthedocs.io/en/latest/.

To get OpenCV running on this **virtualenv**, we need to install the NumPy package:

```
$(virtual_env) pip install numpy
```

Following all the previous steps, just add the following three flags on compilation by cmake (pay attention that flag CMAKE_INSTALL_PREFIX is being redefined):

```
$(<env_name>) > cmake ...
-D CMAKE_INSTALL_PREFIX=~/.virtualenvs/<env_name> \
-D PYTHON_EXECUTABLE=~/.virtualenvs/<env_name>/bin/python
-D PYTHON_PACKAGES_PATH=~/.virtualenvs/<env_name>/lib/python<version>/site-
packages ...
```

Let's make sure that it's installed correctly. Open up the Python shell and type the following:

```
> import cv2
```

If you don't see any errors, you are good to go.

Troubleshooting

If the `cv2` library was not found, identify where the library was compiled. It should be located at `/usr/local/lib/python2.7/site-packages/cv2.so`. If that is the case, make sure your Python version matches the one package that has been stored, otherwise just move it into the according `site-packages` folder of Python, including same for virtualenvs.

During `cmake` command execution, try to join `-DMAKE`... and the rest of the `-D` lines. Moreover, if execution fails during the compiling process, some libraries might be missing from the OS initial requirements. Make sure you installed them all.

You can find an official tutorial about how to install the latest version of OpenCV on Linux at the following website: `http://docs.opencv.org/trunk/d7/d9f/tutorial_linux_install.html`.

If you are trying to compile using Python 3, and `cv2.so` is not installed, make sure you installed OS dependency Python 3 and NumPy.

OpenCV documentation

OpenCV official documentation is at `http://docs.opencv.org/`. There are three documentation categories: Doxygen, Sphinx, and Javadoc.

In order to obtain a better understanding of how to use each of the functions used during this book, we encourage you to open one of those doc pages and research the different uses of each OpenCV library method used in our examples. As a suggestion, Doxygen documentation has more accurate and extended information about the use of OpenCV.

Reading, displaying, and saving images

Let's see how we can load an image in OpenCV-Python. Create a file named `first_program.py` and open it in your favorite code editor. Create a folder named `images` in the current folder, and make sure that you have an image named `input.jpg` in that folder.

Once you do that, add the following lines to that Python file:

```
import cv2
img = cv2.imread('./images/input.jpg')
```

```
cv2.imshow('Input image', img)
cv2.waitKey()
```

If you run the preceding program, you will see an image being displayed in a new window.

What just happened?

Let's understand the previous piece of code, line by line. In the first line, we are importing the OpenCV library. We need this for all the functions we will be using in the code. In the second line, we are reading the image and storing it in a variable. OpenCV uses NumPy data structures to store the images. You can learn more about NumPy at `http://www.numpy.org`.

So if you open up the Python shell and type the following, you will see the datatype printed on the terminal:

```
> import cv2
> img = cv2.imread('./images/input.jpg')
> type(img)
<type 'numpy.ndarray'>
```

In the next line, we display the image in a new window. The first argument in `cv2.imshow` is the name of the window. The second argument is the image you want to display.

You must be wondering why we have the last line here. The function, `cv2.waitKey()`, is used in OpenCV for keyboard binding. It takes a number as an argument, and that number indicates the time in milliseconds. Basically, we use this function to wait for a specified duration, until we encounter a keyboard event. The program stops at this point, and waits for you to press any key to continue. If we don't pass any argument, or if we pass as the argument, this function will wait for a keyboard event indefinitely.

The last statement, `cv2.waitKey(n)`, performs the rendering of the image loaded in the step before. It takes a number that indicates the time in milliseconds of rendering. Basically, we use this function to wait for a specified duration until we encounter a keyboard event. The program stops at this point, and waits for you to press any key to continue. If we don't pass any argument, or if we pass 0 as the argument, this function waits for a keyboard event indefinitely.

Loading and saving an image

OpenCV provides multiple ways of loading an image. Let's say we want to load a color image in grayscale mode, we can do that using the following piece of code:

```
import cv2
gray_img = cv2.imread('images/input.jpg', cv2.IMREAD_GRAYSCALE)
cv2.imshow('Grayscale', gray_img)
cv2.waitKey()
```

Here, we are using the ImreadFlag, as cv2.IMREAD_GRAYSCALE, and loading the image in grayscale mode, although you may find more read modes in the official documentation.

You can see the image displayed in the new window. Here is the input image:

Following is the corresponding grayscale image:

We can save this image as a file as well:

```
cv2.imwrite('images/output.jpg', gray_img)
```

This will save the grayscale image as an output file named `output.jpg`. Make sure you get comfortable with reading, displaying, and saving images in OpenCV, because we will be doing this quite a bit during the course of this book.

Changing image format

We can save this image as a file as well, and change the original image format to PNG:

```
import cv2
img = cv2.imread('images/input.jpg')
cv2.imwrite('images/output.png', img, [cv2.IMWRITE_PNG_COMPRESSION])
```

The `imwrite()` method will save the grayscale image as an output file named `output.png`. This is done using PNG compression with the help of *ImwriteFlag* and `cv2.IMWRITE_PNG_COMPRESSION`. The *ImwriteFlag* allows the output image to change the format, or even the image quality.

Image color spaces

In computer vision and image processing, color space refers to a specific way of organizing colors. A color space is actually a combination of two things, a color model and a mapping function. The reason we want color models is because it helps us in representing pixel values using tuples. The mapping function maps the color model to the set of all possible colors that can be represented.

There are many different color spaces that are useful. Some of the more popular color spaces are RGB, YUV, HSV, Lab, and so on. Different color spaces provide different advantages. We just need to pick the color space that's right for the given problem. Let's take a couple of color spaces and see what information they provide:

- **RGB**: Probably the most popular color space. It stands for Red, Green, and Blue. In this color space, each color is represented as a weighted combination of red, green, and blue. So every pixel value is represented as a tuple of three numbers corresponding to red, green, and blue. Each value ranges between 0 and 255.

- **YUV**: Even though RGB is good for many purposes, it tends to be very limited for many real-life applications. People started thinking about different methods to separate the intensity information from the color information. Hence, they came up with the YUV color space. Y refers to the luminance or intensity, and U/V channels represent color information. This works well in many applications because the human visual system perceives intensity information very differently from color information.

- **HSV**: As it turned out, even YUV was still not good enough for some applications. So people started thinking about how humans perceive color, and they came up with the HSV color space. HSV stands for Hue, Saturation, and Value. This is a cylindrical system where we separate three of the most primary properties of colors and represent them using different channels. This is closely related to how the human visual system understands color. This gives us a lot of flexibility as to how we can handle images.

Converting color spaces

Considering all the color spaces, there are around 190 conversion options available in OpenCV. If you want to see a list of all available flags, go to the Python shell and type the following:

```
import cv2
print([x for x in dir(cv2) if x.startswith('COLOR_')])
```

You will see a list of options available in OpenCV for converting from one color space to another. We can pretty much convert any color space to any other color space. Let's see how we can convert a color image to a grayscale image:

```
import cv2
img = cv2.imread('./images/input.jpg', cv2.IMREAD_COLOR)
gray_img = cv2.cvtColor(img, cv2.COLOR_RGB2GRAY)
cv2.imshow('Grayscale image', gray_img)
cv2.waitKey()
```

What just happened?

We use the cvtColor function to convert color spaces. The first argument is the input image and the second argument specifies the color space conversion.

Splitting image channels

You can convert to YUV by using the following flag:

```
yuv_img = cv2.cvtColor(img, cv2.COLOR_BGR2YUV)
```

The image will look something like the following one:

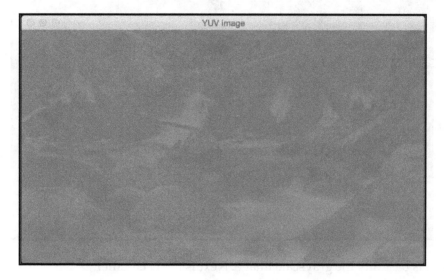

This may look like a deteriorated version of the original image, but it's not. Let's separate out the three channels:

```
# Alternative 1
y,u,v = cv2.split(yuv_img)
cv2.imshow('Y channel', y)
cv2.imshow('U channel', u)
cv2.imshow('V channel', v)
cv2.waitKey()

# Alternative 2 (Faster)
cv2.imshow('Y channel', yuv_img[:, :, 0])
cv2.imshow('U channel', yuv_img[:, :, 1])
cv2.imshow('V channel', yuv_img[:, :, 2])
cv2.waitKey()
```

Since `yuv_img` is a NumPy (which provides dimensional selection operators), we can separate out the three channels by slicing it. If you look at `yuv_img.shape`, you will see that it is a 3D array. So once you run the preceding piece of code, you will see three different images. Following is the **Y channel**:

The channel is basically the grayscale image. Next is the **U channel**:

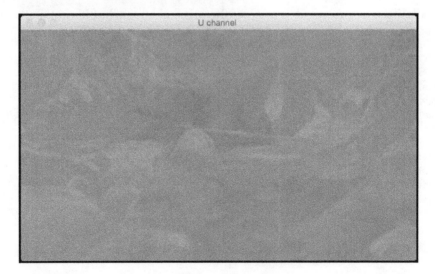

And lastly, the **V channel**:

As we can see here, the channel is the same as the grayscale image. It represents the intensity values, and channels represent the color information.

Merging image channels

Now we are going to read an image, split it into separate channels, and merge them to see how different effects can be obtained out of different combinations:

```
img = cv2.imread('./images/input.jpg', cv2.IMREAD_COLOR)
g,b,r = cv2.split(img)
gbr_img = cv2.merge((g,b,r))
rbr_img = cv2.merge((r,b,r))
cv2.imshow('Original', img)
cv2.imshow('GRB', gbr_img)
cv2.imshow('RBR', rbr_img)
cv2.waitKey()
```

Here we can see how channels can be recombined to obtain different color intensities:

In this one, the red channel is used twice so the reds are more intense:

This should give you a basic idea of how to convert between color spaces. You can play around with more color spaces to see what the images look like. We will discuss the relevant color spaces as and when we encounter them during subsequent chapters.

Image translation

In this section, we will discuss shifting an image. Let's say we want to move the image within our frame of reference. In computer vision terminology, this is referred to as translation. Let's go ahead and see how we can do that:

```
import cv2
import numpy as np
img = cv2.imread('images/input.jpg')
num_rows, num_cols = img.shape[:2]
translation_matrix = np.float32([ [1,0,70], [0,1,110] ])
img_translation = cv2.warpAffine(img, translation_matrix, (num_cols,
num_rows), cv2.INTER_LINEAR)
cv2.imshow('Translation', img_translation)
cv2.waitKey()
```

If you run the preceding code, you will see something like the following:

What just happened?

To understand the preceding code, we need to understand how warping works. Translation basically means that we are shifting the image by adding/subtracting the x and y coordinates. In order to do this, we need to create a transformation matrix, as follows:

$$T = \begin{bmatrix} 1 & 0 & t_x \\ 0 & 1 & t_y \end{bmatrix}$$

Here, the t_x and t_y values are the x and y translation values; that is, the image will be moved by x units to the right, and by y units downwards. So once we create a matrix like this, we can use the function, `warpAffine`, to apply it to our image. The third argument in `warpAffine` refers to the number of rows and columns in the resulting image. As follows, it passes `InterpolationFlags` which defines combination of interpolation methods.

Since the number of rows and columns is the same as the original image, the resultant image is going to get cropped. The reason for this is we didn't have enough space in the output when we applied the translation matrix. To avoid cropping, we can do something like this:

```
img_translation = cv2.warpAffine(img, translation_matrix,
    (num_cols + 70, num_rows + 110))
```

If you replace the corresponding line in our program with the preceding line, you will see the following image:

Let's say you want to move the image to the middle of a bigger image frame; we can do something like this by carrying out the following:

```
import cv2
import numpy as np
img = cv2.imread('images/input.jpg')
num_rows, num_cols = img.shape[:2]
translation_matrix = np.float32([ [1,0,70], [0,1,110] ])
img_translation = cv2.warpAffine(img, translation_matrix, (num_cols + 70,
num_rows + 110))
translation_matrix = np.float32([ [1,0,-30], [0,1,-50] ])
img_translation = cv2.warpAffine(img_translation, translation_matrix,
(num_cols + 70 + 30, num_rows + 110 + 50))
cv2.imshow('Translation', img_translation)
cv2.waitKey()
```

If you run the preceding code, you will see an image like the following:

Moreover, there are two more arguments, `borderMode` and `borderValue`, that allow you to fill up the empty borders of the translation with a pixel extrapolation method:

```
import cv2
import numpy as np
img = cv2.imread('./images/input.jpg')
num_rows, num_cols = img.shape[:2]
translation_matrix = np.float32([ [1,0,70], [0,1,110] ])
img_translation = cv2.warpAffine(img, translation_matrix, (num_cols,
num_rows), cv2.INTER_LINEAR, cv2.BORDER_WRAP, 1)
cv2.imshow('Translation', img_translation)
cv2.waitKey()
```

Image rotation

In this section, we will see how to rotate a given image by a certain angle. We can do it using the following piece of code:

```
import cv2
import numpy as np
img = cv2.imread('images/input.jpg')num_rows, num_cols = img.shape[:2]
rotation_matrix = cv2.getRotationMatrix2D((num_cols/2, num_rows/2), 30,
0.7)
img_rotation = cv2.warpAffine(img, rotation_matrix, (num_cols, num_rows))
cv2.imshow('Rotation', img_rotation)
cv2.waitKey()
```

If you run the preceding code, you will see an image like this:

What just happened?

Using `getRotationMatrix2D`, we can specify the center point around which the image would be rotated as the first argument, then the angle of rotation in degrees, and a scaling factor for the image at the end. We use 0.7 to shrink the image by 30% so it fits in the frame.

In order to understand this, let's see how we handle rotation mathematically. Rotation is also a form of transformation, and we can achieve it by using the following transformation matrix:

$$R = \begin{bmatrix} \cos\theta & -\sin\theta \\ \sin\theta & \cos\theta \end{bmatrix}$$

Here, θ is the angle of rotation in the counterclockwise direction. OpenCV provides finer control over the creation of this matrix through the `getRotationMatrix2D` function. We can specify the point around which the image would be rotated, the angle of rotation in degrees, and a scaling factor for the image. Once we have the transformation matrix, we can use the warpAffine function to apply this matrix to any image.

As we can see from the previous figure, the image content goes out of bounds and gets cropped. In order to prevent this, we need to provide enough space in the output image.

Let's go ahead and do that using the translation functionality we discussed earlier:

```
import cv2
import numpy as np

img = cv2.imread('images/input.jpg')
num_rows, num_cols = img.shape[:2]

translation_matrix = np.float32([ [1,0,int(0.5*num_cols)],
[0,1,int(0.5*num_rows)] ])
rotation_matrix = cv2.getRotationMatrix2D((num_cols, num_rows), 30, 1)

img_translation = cv2.warpAffine(img, translation_matrix, (2*num_cols,
2*num_rows))
img_rotation = cv2.warpAffine(img_translation, rotation_matrix,
(num_cols*2, num_rows*2))

cv2.imshow('Rotation', img_rotation)
cv2.waitKey()
```

If we run the preceding code, we will see something like this:

Image scaling

In this section, we will discuss resizing an image. This is one of the most common operations in computer vision. We can resize an image using a scaling factor, or we can resize it to a particular size. Let's see how to do that:

```
import cv2
img = cv2.imread('images/input.jpg')
img_scaled = cv2.resize(img,None,fx=1.2, fy=1.2, interpolation =
```

```
cv2.INTER_LINEAR)
cv2.imshow('Scaling - Linear Interpolation', img_scaled)
img_scaled = cv2.resize(img,None,fx=1.2, fy=1.2, interpolation =
cv2.INTER_CUBIC)
cv2.imshow('Scaling - Cubic Interpolation', img_scaled)
img_scaled = cv2.resize(img,(450, 400), interpolation = cv2.INTER_AREA)
cv2.imshow('Scaling - Skewed Size', img_scaled)
cv2.waitKey()
```

What just happened?

Whenever we resize an image, there are multiple ways to fill in the pixel values. When we are enlarging an image, we need to fill up the pixel values in between pixel locations. When we are shrinking an image, we need to take the best representative value. When we are scaling by a non-integer value, we need to interpolate values appropriately, so that the quality of the image is maintained. There are multiple ways to do interpolation. If we are enlarging an image, it's preferable to use linear or cubic interpolation. If we are shrinking an image, it's preferable to use area-based interpolation. Cubic interpolation is computationally more complex, and hence slower than linear interpolation. However, the quality of the resulting image will be higher.

OpenCV provides a function called resize to achieve image scaling. If you don't specify a size (by using None), then it expects the *x* and *y* scaling factors. In our example, the image will be enlarged by a factor of 1.2. If we do the same enlargement using cubic interpolation, we can see that the quality improves, as seen in the following figure. The following screenshot shows what linear interpolation looks like:

Here is the corresponding cubic interpolation:

If we want to resize it to a particular size, we can use the format shown in the last resize instance. We can basically skew the image and resize it to whatever size we want. The output will look something like the following:

Affine transformations

In this section, we will discuss the various generalized geometrical transformations of 2D images. We have been using the function `warpAffine` quite a bit over the last couple of sections, it's about time we understood what's happening underneath.

Before talking about affine transformations, let's learn what Euclidean transformations are. Euclidean transformations are a type of geometric transformation that preserve length and angle measures. If we take a geometric shape and apply Euclidean transformation to it, the shape will remain unchanged. It might look rotated, shifted, and so on, but the basic structure will not change. So technically, lines will remain lines, planes will remain planes, squares will remain squares, and circles will remain circles.

Coming back to affine transformations, we can say that they are generalizations of Euclidean transformations. Under the realm of affine transformations, lines will remain lines, but squares might become rectangles or parallelograms. Basically, affine transformations don't preserve lengths and angles.

In order to build a general affine transformation matrix, we need to define the control points. Once we have these control points, we need to decide where we want them to be mapped. In this particular situation, all we need are three points in the source image, and three points in the output image. Let's see how we can convert an image into a parallelogram-like image:

```
import cv2
import numpy as np
img = cv2.imread('images/input.jpg')
rows, cols = img.shape[:2]
src_points = np.float32([[0,0], [cols-1,0], [0,rows-1]])
dst_points = np.float32([[0,0], [int(0.6*(cols-1)),0],
[int(0.4*(cols-1)),rows-1]])
affine_matrix = cv2.getAffineTransform(src_points, dst_points)
img_output = cv2.warpAffine(img, affine_matrix, (cols,rows))
cv2.imshow('Input', img)
cv2.imshow('Output', img_output)
cv2.waitKey()
```

What just happened?

As we discussed earlier, we are defining control points. We just need three points to get the affine transformation matrix. We want the three points in `src_points` to be mapped to the corresponding points in `dst_points`. We are mapping the points as shown in the following image:

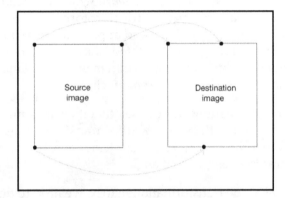

To get the transformation matrix, we have a function called in OpenCV. Once we have the affine transformation matrix, we use the function to apply this matrix to the input image.

Following is the input image:

If you run the preceding code, the output will look something like this:

We can also get the mirror image of the input image. We just need to change the control points in the following way:

```
src_points = np.float32([[0,0], [cols-1,0], [0,rows-1]])
dst_points = np.float32([[cols-1,0], [0,0], [cols-1,rows-1]])
```

Here, the mapping looks something like this:

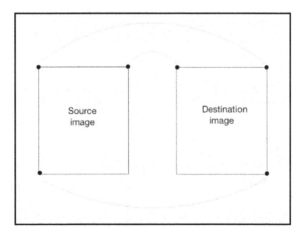

If you replace the corresponding lines in our affine transformation code with these two lines, you will get the following result:

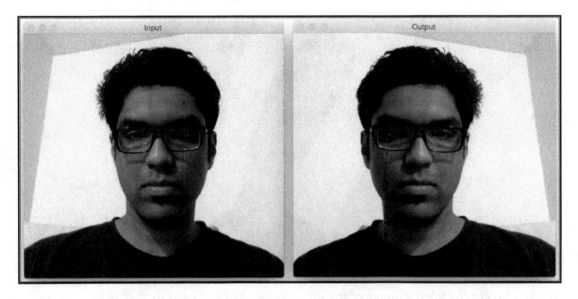

Projective transformations

Affine transformations are nice, but they impose certain restrictions. A projective transformation, on the other hand, gives us more freedom. In order to understand projective transformations, we need to understand how projective geometry works. We basically describe what happens to an image when the point of view is changed. For example, if you are standing right in front of a sheet of paper with a square drawn on it, it will look like a square.

Now, if you start tilting that sheet of paper, the square will start looking more and more like a trapezoid. Projective transformations allow us to capture this dynamic in a nice mathematical way. These transformations preserve neither sizes nor angles, but they do preserve incidence and cross-ratio.

 You can read more about incidence and cross-ratio at `http://en.wikipedia.org/wiki/Incidence_(geometry)` and `http://en.wikipedia.org/wiki/Cross-ratio`.

Now that we know what projective transformations are, let's see if we can extract more information here. We can say that any two images on a given plane are related by a homography. As long as they are in the same plane, we can transform anything into anything else. This has many practical applications such as augmented reality, image rectification, image registration, or the computation of camera motion between two images. Once the camera rotation and translation have been extracted from an estimated homography matrix, this information may be used for navigation, or to insert models of 3D objects into an image or video. This way, they are rendered with the correct perspective, and it will look like they were part of the original scene.

Let's go ahead and see how to do this:

```
import cv2
import numpy as np
img = cv2.imread('images/input.jpg')
rows, cols = img.shape[:2]
src_points = np.float32([[0,0], [cols-1,0], [0,rows-1], [cols-1,rows-1]])
dst_points = np.float32([[0,0], [cols-1,0], [int(0.33*cols),rows-1],
[int(0.66*cols),rows-1]])
projective_matrix = cv2.getPerspectiveTransform(src_points, dst_points)
img_output = cv2.warpPerspective(img, projective_matrix, (cols,rows))
cv2.imshow('Input', img)
cv2.imshow('Output', img_output)
cv2.waitKey()
```

If you run the preceding code you will see the funny-looking output, such as the following screenshot:

What just happened?

We can choose four control points in the source image and map them to the destination image. Parallel lines will not remain parallel lines after the transformation. We use a function called `getPerspectiveTransform` to get the transformation matrix.

Let's apply a couple of fun effects using projective transformation, and see what they look like. All we need to do is change the control points to get different effects.

Here's an example:

The control points are as follows:

```
src_points = np.float32([[0,0], [0,rows-1], [cols/2,0],[cols/2,rows-1]])
dst_points = np.float32([[0,100], [0,rows-101],
[cols/2,0],[cols/2,rows-1]])
```

As an exercise, you should map the preceding points on a plane, and see how the points are mapped (just like we did earlier, while discussing affine transformations). You will get a good understanding about the mapping system, and you can create your own control points. If we want to obtain the same effect on the *y* axis we could apply the previous transformation.

Image warping

Let's have some more fun with the images and see what else we can achieve. Projective transformations are pretty flexible, but they still impose some restrictions on how we can transform the points. What if we want to do something completely random? We need more control, right? It just so happens we can do that as well. We just need to create our own mapping, and it's not that difficult. Following are a few effects that you can achieve with image warping:

Here is the code to create these effects:

```
import cv2
import numpy as np
import math

img = cv2.imread('images/input.jpg', cv2.IMREAD_GRAYSCALE)
rows, cols = img.shape

#####################
```

```
# Vertical wave

img_output = np.zeros(img.shape, dtype=img.dtype)

for i in range(rows):
    for j in range(cols):
        offset_x = int(25.0 * math.sin(2 * 3.14 * i / 180))
        offset_y = 0
        if j+offset_x < rows:
            img_output[i,j] = img[i,(j+offset_x)%cols]
        else:
            img_output[i,j] = 0

cv2.imshow('Input', img)
cv2.imshow('Vertical wave', img_output)


####################
# Horizontal wave

img_output = np.zeros(img.shape, dtype=img.dtype)

for i in range(rows):
    for j in range(cols):
        offset_x = 0
        offset_y = int(16.0 * math.sin(2 * 3.14 * j / 150))
        if i+offset_y < rows:
            img_output[i,j] = img[(i+offset_y)%rows,j]
        else:
            img_output[i,j] = 0

cv2.imshow('Horizontal wave', img_output)


####################
# Both horizontal and vertical

img_output = np.zeros(img.shape, dtype=img.dtype)

for i in range(rows):
    for j in range(cols):
        offset_x = int(20.0 * math.sin(2 * 3.14 * i / 150))
        offset_y = int(20.0 * math.cos(2 * 3.14 * j / 150))
        if i+offset_y < rows and j+offset_x < cols:
            img_output[i,j] = img[(i+offset_y)%rows,(j+offset_x)%cols]
        else:
            img_output[i,j] = 0

cv2.imshow('Multidirectional wave', img_output)
```

```
####################
# Concave effect

img_output = np.zeros(img.shape, dtype=img.dtype)

for i in range(rows):
    for j in range(cols):
        offset_x = int(128.0 * math.sin(2 * 3.14 * i / (2*cols)))
        offset_y = 0
        if j+offset_x < cols:
            img_output[i,j] = img[i,(j+offset_x)%cols]
        else:
            img_output[i,j] = 0

cv2.imshow('Concave', img_output)

cv2.waitKey()
```

Summary

In this chapter, we learned how to install OpenCV-Python on various platforms. We discussed how to read, display, and save images. We talked about the importance of various color spaces, and how we can convert to multiple color spaces, splitting and merging them. We learned how to apply geometric transformations to images, and understood how to use those transformations to achieve cool geometric effects. We discussed the underlying formulation of transformation matrices, and how we can formulate different kinds of transformations based on our needs. We learned how to select control points based on the required geometric transformation. We discussed projective transformations and learned how to use image warping to achieve any given geometric effect.

In the next chapter, we are going to discuss edge detection and image filtering. We can apply a lot of visual effects using image filters, and the underlying formation gives us a lot of freedom to manipulate images in creative ways.

2
Detecting Edges and Applying Image Filters

In this chapter, we are going to see how to apply cool visual effects to images. We will learn how to use fundamental image processing operators, discuss edge detection, and see how we can use image filters to apply various effects to photos.

By the end of this chapter, you will know:

- What 2D convolution is, and how to use it
- How to blur an image
- How to detect edges in an image
- How to apply motion blur to an image
- How to sharpen and emboss an image
- How to erode and dilate an image
- How to create a vignette filter
- How to enhance image contrast

2D convolution

Convolution is a fundamental operation in image processing. We basically apply a mathematical operator to each pixel, and change its value in some way. To apply this mathematical operator, we use another matrix called a **kernel**. The kernel is usually much smaller in size than the input image. For each pixel in the image, we take the kernel and place it on top so that the center of the kernel coincides with the pixel under consideration. We then multiply each value in the kernel matrix with the corresponding values in the image, and then sum it up. This is the new value that will be applied to this position in the output image.

Here, the kernel is called the image filter and the process of applying this kernel to the given image is called image filtering. The output obtained after applying the kernel to the image is called the filtered image. Depending on the values in the kernel, it performs different functions such as blurring, detecting edges, and so on. The following figure should help you visualize the image filtering operation:

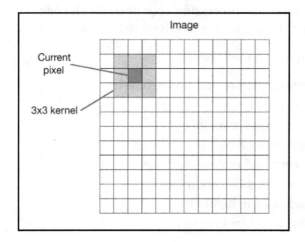

Let's start with the simplest case, which is the identity kernel. This kernel doesn't really change the input image. If we consider a 3x3 identity kernel, it looks something like the following:

$$I = \begin{bmatrix} 0 & 0 & 0 \\ 0 & 1 & 0 \\ 0 & 0 & 0 \end{bmatrix}$$

Blurring

Blurring refers to averaging the pixel values within a neighborhood. This is also called a **low pass filter**. A low pass filter is a filter that allows low frequencies, and blocks higher frequencies. Now, the next question that comes to our mind is: what does frequency mean in an image? Well, in this context, frequency refers to the rate of change of pixel values. So we can say that the sharp edges would be high-frequency content because the pixel values change rapidly in that region. Going by that logic, plain areas would be low-frequency content. Going by this definition, a low pass filter would try to smooth the edges.

A simple way to build a low pass filter is by uniformly averaging the values in the neighborhood of a pixel. We can choose the size of the kernel depending on how much we want to smooth the image, and it will correspondingly have different effects. If you choose a bigger size, then you will be averaging over a larger area. This tends to increase the smoothing effect. Let's see what a 3x3 low pass filter kernel looks like:

$$ L = \frac{1}{9} \begin{bmatrix} 1 & 1 & 1 \\ 1 & 1 & 1 \\ 1 & 1 & 1 \end{bmatrix} $$

We are dividing the matrix by 9 because we want the values to sum up to one. This is called **normalization**, and it's important because we don't want to artificially increase the intensity value at that pixel's location. So, you should normalize the kernel before applying it to an image. Normalization is a really important concept, and it is used in a variety of scenarios, so you should read a couple of tutorials online to get a good grasp on it.

Here is the code to apply this low pass filter to an image:

```
import cv2
import numpy as np

img = cv2.imread('images/input.jpg')
rows, cols = img.shape[:2]

kernel_identity = np.array([[0,0,0], [0,1,0], [0,0,0]])
kernel_3x3 = np.ones((3,3), np.float32) / 9.0 # Divide by 9 to normalize
the kernel
kernel_5x5 = np.ones((5,5), np.float32) / 25.0 # Divide by 25 to normalize
the kernel

cv2.imshow('Original', img)

# value -1 is to maintain source image depth
```

```
output = cv2.filter2D(img, -1, kernel_identity)
cv2.imshow('Identity filter', output)

output = cv2.filter2D(img, -1, kernel_3x3)
cv2.imshow('3x3 filter', output)

output = cv2.filter2D(img, -1, kernel_5x5)
cv2.imshow('5x5 filter', output)

cv2.waitKey(0)
```

If you run the preceding code, you will see something like this:

Size of the kernel versus blurriness

In the preceding code, we are generating different kernels in the code, which are `kernel_identity`, `kernel_3x3`, and `kernel_5x5`. We use the function, `filter2D`, to apply these kernels to the input image. If you look at the images carefully, you can see that they keep getting blurrier as we increase the kernel size. The reason for this is because when we increase the kernel size, we are averaging over a larger area. This tends to have a larger blurring effect.

An alternative way of doing this would be by using the OpenCV function, `blur`. If you don't want to generate the kernels yourself, you can just use this function directly. We can call it using the following line of code:

```
output = cv2.blur(img, (3,3))
```

This will apply the 3x3 kernel to the input and give you the output directly.

Motion blur

When we apply the motion blurring effect, it will look like you captured the picture while moving in a particular direction. For example, you can make an image look like it was captured from a moving car.

The input and output images will look like the following ones:

Following is the code to achieve this motion blurring effect:

```
import cv2
import numpy as np

img = cv2.imread('images/input.jpg')
cv2.imshow('Original', img)

size = 15

# generating the kernel
kernel_motion_blur = np.zeros((size, size))
kernel_motion_blur[int((size-1)/2), :] = np.ones(size)
kernel_motion_blur = kernel_motion_blur / size

# applying the kernel to the input image
output = cv2.filter2D(img, -1, kernel_motion_blur)

cv2.imshow('Motion Blur', output)
cv2.waitKey(0)
```

Under the hood

We are reading the image as usual. We are then constructing a motion `blur` kernel. A motion blur kernel averages the pixel values in a particular direction. It's like a directional low pass filter. A 3x3 horizontal motion-blurring kernel would look this:

$$M = \begin{bmatrix} 0 & 0 & 0 \\ 1 & 1 & 1 \\ 0 & 0 & 0 \end{bmatrix}$$

This will blur the image in a horizontal direction. You can pick any direction and it will work accordingly. The amount of blurring will depend on the size of the kernel. So, if you want to make the image blurrier, just pick a bigger size for the kernel. To see the full effect, we have taken a 15x15 kernel in the preceding code. We then use `filter2D` to apply this kernel to the input image, to obtain the motion-blurred output.

Sharpening

Applying the sharpening filter will sharpen the edges in the image. This filter is very useful when we want to enhance the edges of an image that's not crisp enough. Here are some images to give you an idea of what the image sharpening process looks like:

As you can see in the preceding figure, the level of sharpening depends on the type of kernel we use. We have a lot of freedom to customize the kernel here, and each kernel will give you a different kind of sharpening. To just sharpen an image, as we are doing in the top-right image in the preceding picture, we would use a kernel like this:

$$M = \begin{bmatrix} -1 & -1 & -1 \\ -1 & 9 & -1 \\ -1 & -1 & -1 \end{bmatrix}$$

If we want to do excessive sharpening, as in the bottom-left image, we would use the following kernel:

$$M = \begin{bmatrix} 1 & 1 & 1 \\ 1 & -7 & 1 \\ 1 & 1 & 1 \end{bmatrix}$$

But the problem with these two kernels is that the output image looks artificially enhanced. If we want our images to look more natural, we would use an edge enhancement filter. The underlying concept remains the same, but we use an approximate Gaussian kernel to build this filter. It will help us smooth the image when we enhance the edges, thus making the image look more natural.

Here is the code to achieve the effects applied in the preceding screenshot:

```
import cv2
import numpy as np

img = cv2.imread('images/input.jpg')
cv2.imshow('Original', img)

# generating the kernels
kernel_sharpen_1 = np.array([[-1,-1,-1], [-1,9,-1], [-1,-1,-1]])
kernel_sharpen_2 = np.array([[1,1,1], [1,-7,1], [1,1,1]])
kernel_sharpen_3 = np.array([[-1,-1,-1,-1,-1],
                             [-1,2,2,2,-1],
                             [-1,2,8,2,-1],
                             [-1,2,2,2,-1],
                             [-1,-1,-1,-1,-1]]) / 8.0

# applying different kernels to the input image
output_1 = cv2.filter2D(img, -1, kernel_sharpen_1)
```

```
output_2 = cv2.filter2D(img, -1, kernel_sharpen_2)
output_3 = cv2.filter2D(img, -1, kernel_sharpen_3)

cv2.imshow('Sharpening', output_1)
cv2.imshow('Excessive Sharpening', output_2)
cv2.imshow('Edge Enhancement', output_3)
cv2.waitKey(0)
```

If you noticed, in the preceding code, we didn't divide the first two kernels by a normalizing factor. The reason for this is that the values inside the kernel already sum up to one, so we are implicitly dividing the matrices by one.

Understanding the pattern

You must have noticed a common pattern in the image filtering code examples. We build a kernel and then use `filter2D` to get the desired output. That's exactly what's happening in this code example as well! You can play around with the values inside the kernel and see if you can get different visual effects. Make sure that you normalize the kernel before applying it, or else the image will look too bright because you are artificially increasing the pixel values in the image.

Embossing

An embossing filter will take an image and convert it to an embossed image. We basically take each pixel, and replace it with a shadow or a highlight. Let's say we are dealing with a relatively plain region in the image. Here, we need to replace it with a plain gray color because there's not much information there. If there is a lot of contrast in a particular region, we will replace it with a white pixel (highlight), or a dark pixel (shadow), depending on the direction in which we are embossing.

This is what it will look like:

Let's take a look at the code and see how to do this:

```
import cv2
import numpy as np

img_emboss_input = cv2.imread('images/input.jpg')

# generating the kernels
kernel_emboss_1 = np.array([[0,-1,-1],
                            [1,0,-1],
                            [1,1,0]])
kernel_emboss_2 = np.array([[-1,-1,0],
                            [-1,0,1],
                            [0,1,1]])
kernel_emboss_3 = np.array([[1,0,0],
                            [0,0,0],
                            [0,0,-1]])
```

```
# converting the image to grayscale
gray_img = cv2.cvtColor(img_emboss_input,cv2.COLOR_BGR2GRAY)

# applying the kernels to the grayscale image and adding the offset to
produce the shadow
output_1 = cv2.filter2D(gray_img, -1, kernel_emboss_1) + 128
output_2 = cv2.filter2D(gray_img, -1, kernel_emboss_2) + 128
output_3 = cv2.filter2D(gray_img, -1, kernel_emboss_3) + 128

cv2.imshow('Input', img_emboss_input)
cv2.imshow('Embossing - South West', output_1)
cv2.imshow('Embossing - South East', output_2)
cv2.imshow('Embossing - North West', output_3)
cv2.waitKey(0)
```

If you run the preceding code, you will see that the output images are embossed. As we can see from the preceding kernels, we are just replacing the current pixel value with the difference of the neighboring pixel values in a particular direction. The embossing effect is achieved by offsetting all the pixel values in the image by 128. This operation adds the highlight/shadow effect to the picture.

Edge detection

The process of edge detection involves detecting sharp edges in the image, and producing a binary image as the output. Typically, we draw white lines on a black background to indicate those edges. We can think of edge detection as a high pass filtering operation. A high pass filter allows high-frequency content to pass through and blocks the low-frequency content. As we discussed earlier, edges are high-frequency content. In edge detection, we want to retain these edges and discard everything else. Hence, we should build a kernel that is the equivalent of a high pass filter.

Let's start with a simple edge detection filter known as the Sobel filter. Since edges can occur in both horizontal and vertical directions, the Sobel filter is composed of the following two kernels:

$$S_x = \begin{bmatrix} -1 & 0 & 1 \\ -2 & 0 & 2 \\ -1 & 0 & 1 \end{bmatrix} \qquad S_y = \begin{bmatrix} -1 & -2 & -1 \\ 0 & 0 & 0 \\ 1 & 2 & 1 \end{bmatrix}$$

The kernel on the left detects horizontal edges and the kernel on the right detects vertical edges. OpenCV provides a function to directly apply the `Sobel` filter to a given image. Here is the code to use Sobel filters to detect edges:

```
import cv2
import numpy as np

img = cv2.imread('images/input_shapes.png', cv2.IMREAD_GRAYSCALE)
rows, cols = img.shape

# It is used depth of cv2.CV_64F.
sobel_horizontal = cv2.Sobel(img, cv2.CV_64F, 1, 0, ksize=5)

# Kernel size can be: 1,3,5 or 7.
sobel_vertical = cv2.Sobel(img, cv2.CV_64F, 0, 1, ksize=5)

cv2.imshow('Original', img)
cv2.imshow('Sobel horizontal', sobel_horizontal)
cv2.imshow('Sobel vertical', sobel_vertical)

cv2.waitKey(0)
```

In the case of 8-bit input images, it will result in truncated derivatives, so depth value `cv2.CV_16U` can be used instead. In case edges are not that well-defined the value of *kernel* can be adjusted, minor to obtain thinner edges and major for the opposite purpose.

The output will look something like the following:

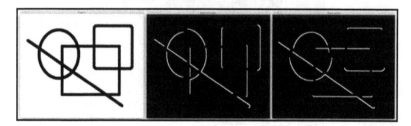

In the preceding figure, the image in the middle is the output of a horizontal edge detector, and the image on the right is the vertical edge detector. As we can see here, the `Sobel` filter detects edges in either a horizontal or vertical direction and it doesn't give us a holistic view of all the edges. To overcome this, we can use the `Laplacian` filter. The advantage of using this filter is that it uses a double derivative in both directions. You can call the function using the following line:

```
laplacian = cv2.Laplacian(img, cv2.CV_64F)
```

The output will look something like the following screenshot:

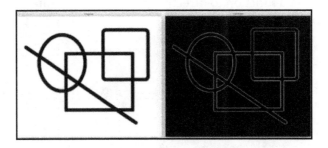

Even though the `Laplacian` kernel worked well in this case, it doesn't always work well. It gives rise to a lot of noise in the output, as shown in the following screenshot. This is where the `Canny` edge detector comes in handy:

As we can see in the preceding images, the `Laplacian` kernel gives rise to a noisy output, which is not exactly useful. To overcome this problem, we use the `Canny` edge detector. To use the `Canny` edge detector, we can use the following function:

```
canny = cv2.Canny(img, 50, 240)
```

As we can see, the quality of the `Canny` edge detector is much better. It takes two numbers as arguments to indicate the thresholds. The second argument is called the **low threshold** value, and the third argument is called the **high threshold** value. If the gradient value is beyond the high threshold value, it is marked as a strong edge. The `Canny` edge detector starts tracking the edge from this point and continues the process until the gradient value falls below the low threshold value. As you increase these thresholds, the weaker edges will be ignored. The output image will be cleaner and sparser. You can play around with the thresholds and see what happens as you increase or decrease their values. The overall formulation is quite deep. You can learn more about it at: http://www.intelligence.tuc. gr/~petrakis/courses/computervision/canny.pdf.

Erosion and dilation

Erosion and **dilation** are morphological image processing operations. Morphological image processing basically deals with modifying geometric structures in the image. These operations are primarily defined for binary images, but we can also use them on grayscale images. Erosion basically strips out the outermost layer of pixels in a structure, whereas dilation adds an extra layer of pixels to a structure.

Let's see what these operations look like:

Following is the code to achieve this:

```
import cv2
import numpy as np

img = cv2.imread('images/input.jpg', 0)

kernel = np.ones((5,5), np.uint8)
```

```
img_erosion = cv2.erode(img, kernel, iterations=1)
img_dilation = cv2.dilate(img, kernel, iterations=1)

cv2.imshow('Input', img)
cv2.imshow('Erosion', img_erosion)
cv2.imshow('Dilation', img_dilation)

cv2.waitKey(0)
```

Afterthought

OpenCV provides functions to directly erode and dilate an image. They are called erode and dilate, respectively. The interesting thing to note is the third argument in these two functions. The number of iterations will determine how much you want to erode/dilate a given image. It basically applies the operation successively to the resultant image. You can take a sample image and play around with this parameter to see what the results look like.

Creating a vignette filter

Using all the information we have, let's see if we can create a nice vignette filter. The output will look something like the following:

Here is the code to achieve this effect:

```
import cv2
import numpy as np

img = cv2.imread('images/input.jpg')
rows, cols = img.shape[:2]

# generating vignette mask using Gaussian kernels
kernel_x = cv2.getGaussianKernel(cols,200)
kernel_y = cv2.getGaussianKernel(rows,200)
kernel = kernel_y * kernel_x.T
mask = 255 * kernel / np.linalg.norm(kernel)
output = np.copy(img)

# applying the mask to each channel in the input image
for i in range(3):
    output[:,:,i] = output[:,:,i] * mask

cv2.imshow('Original', img)
cv2.imshow('Vignette', output)
cv2.waitKey(0)
```

What's happening underneath?

The vignette filter basically focuses the brightness on a particular part of the image and the other parts look faded. In order to achieve this, we need to filter out each channel in the image using a Gaussian kernel. OpenCV provides a function to do this, which is called getGaussianKernel. We need to build a 2D kernel whose size matches the size of the image. The second parameter of the function, getGaussianKernel, is interesting. It is the standard deviation of the Gaussian, and it controls the radius of the bright central region. You can play around with this parameter and see how it affects the output.

Once we build the 2D kernel, we need to build a mask by normalizing this kernel and scaling it up, as shown in the following line:

```
mask = 255 * kernel / np.linalg.norm(kernel)
```

This is an important step because if you don't scale it up, the image will look black. This happens because all the pixel values will be close to zero after you superimpose the mask on the input image. After this, we iterate through all the color channels and apply the mask to each channel.

How do we move the focus around?

We now know how to create a vignette filter that focuses on the center of the image. Let's say we want to achieve the same vignette effect, but we want to focus on a different region in the image, as shown in the following figure:

All we need to do is build a bigger Gaussian kernel, and make sure that the peak coincides with the region of interest. Following is the code to achieve this:

```
import cv2
import numpy as np

img = cv2.imread('images/input.jpg')
rows, cols = img.shape[:2]

# generating vignette mask using Gaussian kernels
kernel_x = cv2.getGaussianKernel(int(1.5*cols),200)
kernel_y = cv2.getGaussianKernel(int(1.5*rows),200)
kernel = kernel_y * kernel_x.T
mask = 255 * kernel / np.linalg.norm(kernel)
mask = mask[int(0.5*rows):, int(0.5*cols):]
output = np.copy(img)

# applying the mask to each channel in the input image
```

```
for i in range(3):
    output[:,:,i] = output[:,:,i] * mask

cv2.imshow('Input', img)
cv2.imshow('Vignette with shifted focus', output)

cv2.waitKey(0)
```

Enhancing the contrast in an image

Whenever we capture images in low-light conditions, the images turn out to be dark. This typically happens when you capture images in the evening, or in a dimly lit room. You must have seen this happen many times! The reason this happens is because the pixel values tend to concentrate near zero when we capture the images under such conditions. When this happens, a lot of details in the image are not clearly visible to the human eye. The human eye likes contrast, and so we need to adjust the contrast to make the image look nice and pleasant. A lot of cameras and photo applications implicitly do this already. We use a process called **histogram equalization** to achieve this.

To give an example, this is what it looks like before and after contrast enhancement:

As we can see here, the input image on the left is really dark. To rectify this, we need to adjust the pixel values so that they are spread across the entire spectrum of values, that is, between 0-255.

Following is the code for adjusting the pixel values:

```
import cv2
import numpy as np

img = cv2.imread('images/input.jpg', 0)

# equalize the histogram of the input image
histeq = cv2.equalizeHist(img)

cv2.imshow('Input', img)
cv2.imshow('Histogram equalized', histeq)
cv2.waitKey(0)
```

Histogram equalization is applicable to grayscale images. OpenCV provides a function, `equalizeHist`, to achieve this effect. As we can see here, the code is pretty straightforward, where we read the image and equalize its histogram to normalize the brightness and increase the contrast of the image.

How do we handle color images?

Now that we know how to equalize the histogram of a grayscale image, you might be wondering how to handle color images. The thing about histogram equalization is that it's a nonlinear process. So, we cannot just separate out the three channels in an RGB image, equalize the histogram separately, and combine them later to form the output image. The concept of histogram equalization is only applicable to the intensity values in the image. So, we have to make sure not to modify the color information when we do this.

In order to handle the histogram equalization of color images, we need to convert it to a color space, where intensity is separated from the color information. YUV is a good example of such a color space, as the YUV model defines a color space in terms of one **Luminance (Y)** and two **Chrominance (UV)** components. Once we convert it to YUV, we just need to equalize the Y-channel and combine it with the other two channels to get the output image.

Following is an example of what it looks like:

Here is the code to achieve histogram equalization for color images:

```
import cv2
import numpy as np

img = cv2.imread('images/input.jpg')

img_yuv = cv2.cvtColor(img, cv2.COLOR_BGR2YUV)

# equalize the histogram of the Y channel
img_yuv[:,:,0] = cv2.equalizeHist(img_yuv[:,:,0])

# convert the YUV image back to RGB format
img_output = cv2.cvtColor(img_yuv, cv2.COLOR_YUV2BGR)

cv2.imshow('Color input image', img)
cv2.imshow('Histogram equalized', img_output)

cv2.waitKey(0)
```

Summary

In this chapter, we learned how to use image filters to apply cool visual effects to images. We discussed the fundamental image processing operators, and how we can use them to build various things. We learned how to detect edges using various methods. We understood the importance of 2D convolution and how we can use it in different scenarios. We discussed how to smooth, motion-blur, sharpen, emboss, erode, and dilate an image. We learned how to create a vignette filter, and how we can change the region of focus as well. We discussed contrast enhancement and how we can use histogram equalization to achieve it.

In the next chapter, we will discuss how to cartoonize a given image.

3
Cartoonizing an Image

In this chapter, we are going to learn how to convert an image into a cartoon-like image. We will learn how to access the webcam and take keyboard/mouse inputs during a live video stream. We will also learn about some advanced image filters, and see how we can use them to, for example, cartoonize an input video.

By the end of this chapter, you will know:

- How to access the webcam
- How to take keyboard and mouse inputs during a live video stream
- How to create an interactive application
- How to use advanced image filters
- How to cartoonize an image

Accessing the webcam

We can build very interesting applications using the live video stream from the webcam. OpenCV provides a video capture object which handles everything related to the opening and closing of the webcam. All we need to do is create that object and keep reading frames from it.

The following code will open the webcam, capture the frames, scale them down by a factor of 2, and then display them in a window. You can press the *Esc* key to exit:

```python
import cv2

cap = cv2.VideoCapture(0)

# Check if the webcam is opened correctly
if not cap.isOpened():
    raise IOError("Cannot open webcam")

while True:
    ret, frame = cap.read()
    frame = cv2.resize(frame, None, fx=0.5, fy=0.5,
interpolation=cv2.INTER_AREA)
    cv2.imshow('Input', frame)

    c = cv2.waitKey(1)
    if c == 27:
        break

cap.release()
cv2.destroyAllWindows()
```

Under the hood

As we can see in the preceding code, we use OpenCV's `VideoCapture` function to create the video capture object cap. Once it's created, we start an infinite loop and keep reading frames from the webcam until we encounter a keyboard interrupt.

In the first line within the while loop, we have the following line:

```python
ret, frame = cap.read()
```

Here, `ret` is a Boolean value returned by the `read` function, and it indicates whether or not the frame was captured successfully. If the frame is captured correctly, it's stored in the variable `frame`. This loop will keep running until we press the *Esc* key. So, we keep checking for a keyboard interrupt in the following line:

```python
if c == 27:
```

As we know, the ASCII value of *Esc* is 27. Once we encounter it, we break the loop and release the video capture object. The line `cap.release()` is important because it gracefully frees the webcam resource so that another application can make use of it.

Extending capture options

In the code discussed earlier, `cv2.VideoCapture(0)` defines the use of the default connected webcam using auto detected reader implementation, but there are multiple options concerning how images are read from the webcam.

At the time of writing this book, with version **OpenCV 3.3.0** there is no proper way to list the available webcams, so in a case where you have multiple webcams connected at the time of running this code, you have to increase the index value of `VideoCapture` until it uses the one that is desired.

It is also possible to force specific reader implementation if multiple are available, such as `cv2.CAP_FFMPEG` and `cv2.CAP_IMAGES`, or everyone starting with `cv2.CAP_*`. You could, for example, use `QuickTime` reader on webcam index 1:

```
cap = cv2.VideoCapture(1 + cv2.CAP_QT) // Webcam index 1 + reader
implementation QuickTime
```

Keyboard inputs

Now that we know how to capture a live video stream from the webcam, let's see how to use the keyboard to interact with the window displaying the video stream:

```
import cv2

def print_howto():
    print("""
        Change color space of the
        input video stream using keyboard controls. The control keys are:
            1. Grayscale - press 'g'
            2. YUV - press 'y'
            3. HSV - press 'h'
    """)

if __name__=='__main__':
    print_howto()
    cap = cv2.VideoCapture(0)

    # Check if the webcam is opened correctly
    if not cap.isOpened():
        raise IOError("Cannot open webcam")

    cur_mode = None
    while True:
```

```
        # Read the current frame from webcam
        ret, frame = cap.read()

        # Resize the captured image
        frame = cv2.resize(frame, None, fx=0.5, fy=0.5,
interpolation=cv2.INTER_AREA)

        c = cv2.waitKey(1)
        if c == 27:
            break
        # Update cur_mode only in case it is different and key was pressed
        # In case a key was not pressed during the iteration result is -1
or 255, depending
        # on library versions
        if c != -1 and c != 255 and c != cur_mode:
            cur_mode = c

        if cur_mode == ord('g'):
            output = cv2.cvtColor(frame, cv2.COLOR_BGR2GRAY)
        elif cur_mode == ord('y'):
            output = cv2.cvtColor(frame, cv2.COLOR_BGR2YUV)
        elif cur_mode == ord('h'):
            output = cv2.cvtColor(frame, cv2.COLOR_BGR2HSV)
        else:
            output = frame
        cv2.imshow('Webcam', output)

    cap.release()
    cv2.destroyAllWindows()
```

Interacting with the application

This program will display the input video stream and wait for the keyboard input to change the color space. If you run the previous program, you will see the window displaying the input video stream from the webcam. If you press G, you will see that the color space of the input stream gets converted to grayscale. If you press Y, the input stream will be converted to YUV color space. Similarly, if you press H, you will see the image being converted to HSV color space.

As we know, we use the function `waitKey()` to listen to keyboard events. As and when we encounter different keystrokes, we take appropriate actions. The reason we are using the function `ord()` is because `waitKey()` returns the ASCII value of the keyboard input; thus, we need to convert the characters into their ASCII form before checking their values.

Mouse inputs

In this section, we will see how to use the mouse to interact with the display window. Let's start with something simple. We will write a program that will detect the quadrant in which the mouse click was detected. Once we detect it, we will highlight that quadrant:

```
import cv2
import numpy as np

def detect_quadrant(event, x, y, flags, param):
    if event == cv2.EVENT_LBUTTONDOWN:
        if x > width/2:
            if y > height/2:
                point_top_left = (int(width/2), int(height/2))
                point_bottom_right = (width-1, height-1)
            else:
                point_top_left = (int(width/2), 0)
                point_bottom_right = (width-1, int(height/2))

        else:
            if y > height/2:
                point_top_left = (0, int(height/2))
                point_bottom_right = (int(width/2), height-1)
            else:
                point_top_left = (0, 0)
                point_bottom_right = (int(width/2), int(height/2))

        img = param["img"]
        # Repaint all in white again
        cv2.rectangle(img, (0,0), (width-1,height-1), (255,255,255), -1)
        # Paint green quadrant
        cv2.rectangle(img, point_top_left, point_bottom_right, (0,100,0),
-1)

if __name__=='__main__':
    width, height = 640, 480
    img = 255 * np.ones((height, width, 3), dtype=np.uint8)
    cv2.namedWindow('Input window')
    cv2.setMouseCallback('Input window', detect_quadrant, {"img": img})

    while True:
        cv2.imshow('Input window', img)
        c = cv2.waitKey(1)
        if c == 27:
            break

    cv2.destroyAllWindows()
```

The output will look something like the following image:

What's happening underneath?

Let's start with the main function in this program. We create a white image on which we are going to click using the mouse. We then create a named window and bind the MouseCallback function to this window. The MouseCallback function is basically the function that will be called when a mouse event is detected. There are many kinds of mouse events, such as clicking, double-clicking, dragging, and so on. In our case, we just want to detect a mouse click. In the detect_quadrant function, we check the first input argument event to see what action was performed. OpenCV provides a set of predefined events, and we can call them using specific keywords. If you want to see a list of all the mouse events, you can go to the Python shell and type the following:

```
>>> import cv2
>>> print([x for x in dir(cv2) if x.startswith('EVENT')])
```

The second and third arguments in the `detect_quadrant` function provide the *X* and *Y* coordinates of the mouse click event. Once we know these coordinates, it's pretty straightforward to determine what quadrant it's in. With this information, we just go ahead and draw a rectangle with the specified color, using `cv2.rectangle()`. This is a very handy function that takes the top left point and the bottom right point to draw a rectangle on an image with the specified color.

Interacting with a live video stream

Let's see how we can use the mouse to interact with a live video stream from the webcam. We can use the mouse to select a region, and then apply a negative film effect on that region, as shown in the following image:

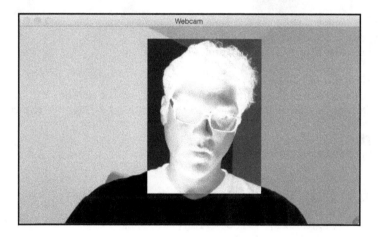

In the following program, we will capture the video stream from the webcam, select a region of interest with the mouse, and then apply this effect:

```
import cv2
import numpy as np

def update_pts(params, x, y):
    global x_init, y_init
    params["top_left_pt"] = (min(x_init, x), min(y_init, y))
    params["bottom_right_pt"] = (max(x_init, x), max(y_init, y))
    img[y_init:y, x_init:x] = 255 - img[y_init:y, x_init:x]

def draw_rectangle(event, x, y, flags, params):
    global x_init, y_init, drawing
    # First click initialize the init rectangle point
```

```
        if event == cv2.EVENT_LBUTTONDOWN:
            drawing = True
            x_init, y_init = x, y
        # Meanwhile mouse button is pressed, update diagonal rectangle point
        elif event == cv2.EVENT_MOUSEMOVE and drawing:
            update_pts(params, x, y)
        # Once mouse botton is release
        elif event == cv2.EVENT_LBUTTONUP:
            drawing = False
            update_pts(params, x, y)

if __name__=='__main__':
    drawing = False
    event_params = {"top_left_pt": (-1, -1), "bottom_right_pt": (-1, -1)}

    cap = cv2.VideoCapture(0)

    # Check if the webcam is opened correctly
    if not cap.isOpened():
        raise IOError("Cannot open webcam")

    cv2.namedWindow('Webcam')
    # Bind draw_rectangle function to every mouse event
    cv2.setMouseCallback('Webcam', draw_rectangle, event_params)

    while True:
        ret, frame = cap.read()
        img = cv2.resize(frame, None, fx=0.5, fy=0.5,
interpolation=cv2.INTER_AREA)
        (x0,y0), (x1,y1) = event_params["top_left_pt"],
event_params["bottom_right_pt"]
        img[y0:y1, x0:x1] = 255 - img[y0:y1, x0:x1]
        cv2.imshow('Webcam', img)

        c = cv2.waitKey(1)
        if c == 27:
            break

    cap.release()
    cv2.destroyAllWindows()
```

If you run the preceding program, you will see a window displaying the video stream. You can just draw a rectangle on the window using your mouse and you will see that region being converted to its negative.

How did we do it?

As we can see in the main function of the program, we initialize a video capture object. We then bind the function `draw_rectangle` with the `MouseCallback` function in the following line:

```
cv2.setMouseCallback('Webcam', draw_rectangle, event_params)
```

We then start an infinite loop and start capturing the video stream. Let's see what is happening in the function `draw_rectangle`; whenever we draw a rectangle using the mouse, we basically have to detect three types of mouse events: mouse click, mouse movement, and mouse button release. This is exactly what we do in this function. Whenever we detect a mouse click event, we initialize the top left point of the rectangle. As we move the mouse, we select the region of interest by keeping the current position as the bottom right point of the rectangle and it is updated at the object passed by reference as a third argument (`event_params`).

Once we have the region of interest, we just invert the pixels to apply the negative film effect. We subtract the current pixel value from 255 and this gives us the desired effect. When the mouse movement stops and a button-up event is detected, we stop updating the bottom right position of the rectangle. We just keep displaying this image until another mouse click event is detected.

Cartoonizing an image

Now that we know how to handle the webcam and keyboard/mouse inputs, let's go ahead and see how to convert a picture into a cartoon-like image. We can convert an image into either a sketch or a colored cartoon image.

The following is an example of what a sketch will look like:

If you apply the cartoonizing effect to the color image, it will look something like this next image:

Let's see how to achieve this:

```python
import cv2
import numpy as np

def print_howto():
    print("""
        Change cartoonizing mode of image:
            1. Cartoonize without Color - press 's'
            2. Cartoonize with Color - press 'c'
    """)

def cartoonize_image(img, ksize=5, sketch_mode=False):
    num_repetitions, sigma_color, sigma_space, ds_factor = 10, 5, 7, 4
    # Convert image to grayscale
    img_gray = cv2.cvtColor(img, cv2.COLOR_BGR2GRAY)

    # Apply median filter to the grayscale image
    img_gray = cv2.medianBlur(img_gray, 7)

    # Detect edges in the image and threshold it
    edges = cv2.Laplacian(img_gray, cv2.CV_8U, ksize=ksize)
    ret, mask = cv2.threshold(edges, 100, 255, cv2.THRESH_BINARY_INV)

    # 'mask' is the sketch of the image
    if sketch_mode:
        return cv2.cvtColor(mask, cv2.COLOR_GRAY2BGR)

    # Resize the image to a smaller size for faster computation
    img_small = cv2.resize(img, None, fx=1.0/ds_factor, fy=1.0/ds_factor,
interpolation=cv2.INTER_AREA)

    # Apply bilateral filter the image multiple times
    for i in range(num_repetitions):
        img_small = cv2.bilateralFilter(img_small, ksize, sigma_color,
sigma_space)

    img_output = cv2.resize(img_small, None, fx=ds_factor, fy=ds_factor,
interpolation=cv2.INTER_LINEAR)

    dst = np.zeros(img_gray.shape)

    # Add the thick boundary lines to the image using 'AND' operator
    dst = cv2.bitwise_and(img_output, img_output, mask=mask)
    return dst

if __name__=='__main__':
    print_howto()
```

```
    cap = cv2.VideoCapture(0)

    cur_mode = None
    while True:
        ret, frame = cap.read()
        frame = cv2.resize(frame, None, fx=0.5, fy=0.5,
interpolation=cv2.INTER_AREA)

        c = cv2.waitKey(1)
        if c == 27:
            break

        if c != -1 and c != 255 and c != cur_mode:
            cur_mode = c

        if cur_mode == ord('s'):
            cv2.imshow('Cartoonize', cartoonize_image(frame, ksize=5,
sketch_mode=True))
        elif cur_mode == ord('c'):
            cv2.imshow('Cartoonize', cartoonize_image(frame, ksize=5,
sketch_mode=False))
        else:
            cv2.imshow('Cartoonize', frame)

    cap.release()
    cv2.destroyAllWindows()
```

Deconstructing the code

When you run the preceding program, you will see a window with a video stream from the webcam. If you press *S*, the video stream will change to sketch mode, and you will see its pencil-like outline. If you press *C*, you will see the color-cartoonized version of the input stream. If you press any other key, it will return to the normal mode.

Let's look at the `cartoonize_image` function and see how we did it. First, we converted the image to a grayscale image, and ran it through a median filter. Median filters are very good at removing salt and pepper noise. This is the kind of noise where you see isolated black or white pixels in the image. It is common in webcams and mobile cameras, so we need to filter it out before we proceed further. To give an example, look at the following images:

As we see in the input image, there are a lot of isolated green pixels. They are lowering the quality of the image and we need to get rid of them. This is where the median filter comes in handy. We just look at the NxN neighborhood around each pixel and pick the median value of those numbers. Since the isolated pixels, in this case, have high values, taking the median value will get rid of these values and also smoothen the image. As you can see in the output image, the median filter got rid of all those isolated pixels and the image looks clean. Following is the code for this:

```
import cv2
import numpy as np

img = cv2.imread('images/input.jpg')
output = cv2.medianBlur(img, ksize=7)
cv2.imshow('Input', img)
cv2.imshow('Median filter', output)
cv2.waitKey()
```

The code is pretty straightforward. We just use the `medianBlur` function to apply the median filter to the input image. The second argument in this function specifies the size of the kernel we are using. The size of the kernel is related to the neighborhood size that we need to consider. You can play around with this parameter and see how it affects the output; remember, the possible values are only odd numbers: 1, 3, 5, 7, and so on.

Coming back to `cartoonize_image`, we proceed to detect the edges on the grayscale image. We need to know where the edges are so that we can create the pencil-line effect. Once we detect the edges, we threshold them so that things become black and white, both literally and metaphorically!

In the next step, we check if the sketch mode is enabled. If it is, then we just convert it into a color image and return it. What if we want the lines to be thicker? Let's say we want to see something like the following image:

As you can see, the lines are thicker than before. To achieve this, replace the `if` code block with the following piece of code:

```
if sketch_mode:
    img_sketch = cv2.cvtColor(mask, cv2.COLOR_GRAY2BGR)
    kernel = np.ones((3,3), np.uint8)
    img_eroded = cv2.erode(img_sketch, kernel, iterations=1)
    return cv2.medianBlur(img_eroded, ksize=5)
```

We are using the `erode` function with a 3x3 kernel here. The reason we have this in place is because it gives us a chance to play with the thickness of the line drawing. Now, you might ask: if we want to increase the thickness of something, shouldn't we be using dilation? Well, this reasoning is right, but there is a small twist here. Note that the foreground is black and the background is white. Erosion and dilation treat white pixels as foreground and black pixels as background. So if we want to increase the thickness of the black foreground, we need to use erosion. After we apply erosion, we just use the median filter to clear out the noise and get the final output.

In the next step, we use bilateral filtering to smoothen the image. Bilateral filtering is an interesting concept, and its performance is much better than a Gaussian filter. The good thing about bilateral filtering is that it preserves the edges, whereas the Gaussian filter smoothens everything out equally. To compare and contrast, let's look at the following input image:

Let's apply the **Gaussian filter** to the previous image:

Now, let's apply the **Bilateral filter** to the input image:

As you can see, the quality is better if we use the bilateral filter. The image looks smooth and the edges look nice and sharp! The code to achieve this is as follows:

```
import cv2
import numpy as np

img = cv2.imread('images/input.jpg')

img_gaussian = cv2.GaussianBlur(img, (13,13), 0) # Gaussian Kernel Size
13x13
img_bilateral = cv2.bilateralFilter(img, 13, 70, 50)

cv2.imshow('Input', img)
cv2.imshow('Gaussian filter', img_gaussian)
cv2.imshow('Bilateral filter', img_bilateral)
cv2.waitKey()
```

If you closely observe the two outputs, you can see that the edges in the Gaussian filtered image look blurred. Usually, we just want to smoothen the rough areas in the image and keep the edges intact. This is where the bilateral filter comes in handy. The Gaussian filter just looks at the immediate neighborhood and averages the pixel values using a Gaussian kernel, applied by the `GaussianBlur` method. The bilateral filter takes this concept to the next level by averaging only those pixels that are similar to each other in intensity. It also takes a color neighborhood metric to see if it can replace the current pixel that is similar in intensity as well. If you look at the function call:

```
img_small = cv2.bilateralFilter(img_small, size, sigma_color,
    sigma_space)
```

The last two arguments here specify the color and space neighborhood. This is the reason the edges look crisp in the output of the bilateral filter. We run this filter multiple times on the image to smoothen it out, to make it look like a cartoon. We then superimpose the pencil-like mask on top of this color image to create a cartoon-like effect.

Summary

In this chapter, we learned how to access the webcam. We discussed how to take the keyboard and mouse inputs during live video streams. We used this knowledge to create an interactive application. We discussed the median and bilateral filters, and talked about the advantages of the bilateral filter over the Gaussian filter. We used all these principles to convert the input image into a sketch-like image, and then cartoonized it.

In the next chapter, we will learn how to detect different body parts in static images, as well as in live videos.

4
Detecting and Tracking Different Body Parts

In this chapter, we are going to learn how to detect and track different body parts in a live video stream. We will start by discussing the face detection pipeline and how it's built from the ground up. We will learn how to use this framework to detect and track other body parts, such as eyes, ears, and mouth.

By the end of this chapter, you will know:

- How to use Haar cascades
- What integral images are
- What adaptive boosting is
- How to detect and track faces in a live video stream
- How to detect and track eyes in a live video stream
- How to automatically overlay sunglasses on top of a person's face
- How to detect eyes, ears, and mouth
- How to detect pupils using shape analysis

Using Haar cascades to detect things

When we say Haar cascades, we are actually talking about cascade classifiers based on Haar features. To understand what this means, we need to take a step back and understand why we need this in the first place. Back in 2001, Paul Viola and Michael Jones came up with a very effective object detection method in their seminal paper. It has become one of the major landmarks in the field of machine learning.

In their paper, they have described a machine learning technique where a boosted cascade of simple classifiers is used to get an overall classifier that performs really well. This way, we can circumvent the process of building a single complex classifier that performs with high accuracy. The reason this is so amazing is because building a robust single-step classifier is a computationally intensive process. Besides, we need a lot of training data to build such a classifier. The model ends up becoming complex and the performance might not be up to the mark.

Let's say we want to detect an object like, say, a pineapple. To solve this, we need to build a machine learning system that will learn what a pineapple looks like. It should be able to tell us if an unknown image contains a pineapple or not. To achieve something like this, we need to train our system. In the realm of machine learning, we have a lot of methods available to train a system. It's a lot like training a dog, except that it won't fetch the ball for you! To train our system, we take a lot of pineapple and non-pineapple images, and then feed them into the system. Here, pineapple images are called **positive images** and the non-pineapple images are called **negative images**.

As far as the training is concerned, there are a lot of routes available. But all the traditional techniques are computationally intensive and result in complex models. We cannot use these models to build a real-time system. Hence, we need to keep the classifier simple. But if we keep the classifier simple, it will not be accurate. The trade-off between speed and accuracy is common in machine learning. We overcome this problem by building a set of simple classifiers and then cascading them together to form a unified classifier that's robust. To make sure that the overall classifier works well, we need to get creative in the cascading step. This is one of the main reasons why the **Viola-Jones** method is so effective.

Coming to the topic of face detection, let's see how to train a system to detect faces. If we want to build a machine learning system, we first need to extract features from all the images. In our case, the machine learning algorithms will use these features to learn what a face looks like. We use Haar features to build our feature vectors. Haar features are simple summations and differences of patches across the image. We do this at multiple image sizes to make sure our system is scale invariant.

 If you are curious, you can learn more about the formulation at: `http://www.cs.ubc.ca/~lowe/425/slides/13-ViolaJones.pdf`

Once we extract these features, we pass it through a cascade of classifiers. We just check all the different rectangular sub-regions and keep discarding the ones that don't have faces in them. This way, we arrive at the final answer quickly to see if a given rectangle contains a face or not.

What are integral images?

If we want to compute Haar features, we will have to compute the summations of many different rectangular regions within the image. If we want to effectively build the feature set, we need to compute these summations at multiple scales. This is a very expensive process! If we want to build a real-time system, we cannot spend so many cycles computing these sums. So we use something called **integral images**:

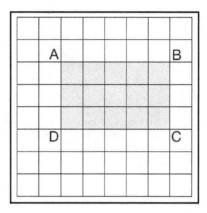

To compute the sum of any rectangle in the image, we don't need to go through all the elements in that rectangular area. Let's say AP indicates the sum of all the elements in the rectangle formed by the top-left point and the point P in the image as the two diagonally opposite corners. So now, if we want to compute the area of the rectangle ABCD, we can use the following formula:

Area of the rectangle ABCD = AC - (AB + AD - AA)

Why do we care about this particular formula? As we discussed earlier, extracting Haar features includes computing the areas of a large number of rectangles in the image at multiple scales. A lot of those computations are repetitive and the overall process is very slow. In fact, it is so slow that we cannot afford to run anything in real time. That's the reason we use this formulation! The good thing about this approach is that we don't have to recalculate anything. All the values for the areas on the right-hand side of this equation are already available. So we just use them to compute the area of any given rectangle and extract the features.

Detecting and tracking faces

OpenCV provides a nice face detection framework. We just need to load the cascade file and use it to detect the faces in an image. Let's see how to do it:

```
import cv2
import numpy as np

face_cascade =
cv2.CascadeClassifier('./cascade_files/haarcascade_frontalface_alt.xml')

cap = cv2.VideoCapture(0)
scaling_factor = 0.5

while True:
    ret, frame = cap.read()
    frame = cv2.resize(frame, None, fx=scaling_factor,
 fy=scaling_factor, interpolation=cv2.INTER_AREA)

    face_rects = face_cascade.detectMultiScale(frame, scaleFactor=1.3,
minNeighbors=3)
    for (x,y,w,h) in face_rects:
        cv2.rectangle(frame, (x,y), (x+w,y+h), (0,255,0), 3)

    cv2.imshow('Face Detector', frame)

    c = cv2.waitKey(1)
    if c == 27:
        break

cap.release()
cv2.destroyAllWindows()
```

If you run the preceding code, the result will look something like the following image:

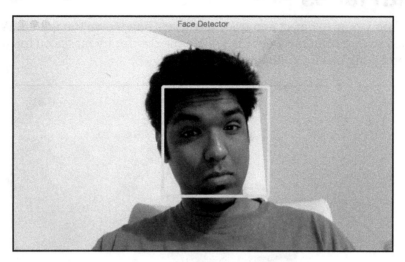

Understanding it better

We need a classifier model that can be used to detect faces in an image. OpenCV provides an XML file that can be used for this purpose. We use the function `CascadeClassifier` to load the XML file. Once we start capturing the input frames from the webcam and use the `detectMultiScale` function to get the bounding boxes for all the faces in the current image, in case frames are not passed in grayscale, this is going to run internally at the method, as grayscaled frames are required to process the detection. The second argument in this function specifies the jump in the scaling factor, as in, if we don't find an image in the current scale, the next size to check will be, in our case, 1.3 times bigger than the current size. The last parameter is a threshold that specifies the minimum number of adjacent rectangles needed to keep the current rectangle. It can be used to increase the robustness of the face detector, in case face recognition does not work as expected, reducing the threshold value to obtain better recognition. In cases where the image suffers some delay due to processing the detection, reduce the size of the scaled frame by 0.4 or 0.3.

Fun with faces

Now that we know how to detect and track faces, let's have some fun with it. When we capture a video stream from the webcam, we can overlay funny masks on top of our faces. It will look something like the following image:

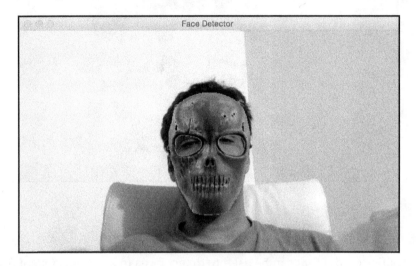

If you are a fan of Hannibal, you can try this one:

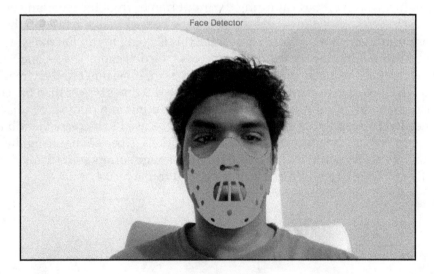

Let's look at the code to see how to overlay the skull mask on top of the face in the input video stream:

```python
import cv2
import numpy as np

face_cascade =
cv2.CascadeClassifier('./cascade_files/haarcascade_frontalface_alt.xml')

face_mask = cv2.imread('./images/mask_hannibal.png')
h_mask, w_mask = face_mask.shape[:2]

if face_cascade.empty():
    raise IOError('Unable to load the face cascade classifier xml file')

cap = cv2.VideoCapture(0)
scaling_factor = 0.5

while True:
    ret, frame = cap.read()
    frame = cv2.resize(frame, None, fx=scaling_factor, fy=scaling_factor,
interpolation=cv2.INTER_AREA)

    face_rects = face_cascade.detectMultiScale(frame, scaleFactor=1.3,
minNeighbors=3)
    for (x,y,w,h) in face_rects:
        if h <= 0 or w <= 0: pass
        # Adjust the height and weight parameters depending on the sizes
and the locations.
        # You need to play around with these to make sure you get it right.
        h, w = int(1.0*h), int(1.0*w)
        y -= int(-0.2*h)
        x = int(x)
        # Extract the region of interest from the image
        frame_roi = frame[y:y+h, x:x+w]
        face_mask_small = cv2.resize(face_mask, (w, h),
interpolation=cv2.INTER_AREA)

        # Convert color image to grayscale and threshold it
        gray_mask = cv2.cvtColor(face_mask_small, cv2.COLOR_BGR2GRAY)
        ret, mask = cv2.threshold(gray_mask, 180, 255,
cv2.THRESH_BINARY_INV)

        # Create an inverse mask
        mask_inv = cv2.bitwise_not(mask)

        try:
```

```
            # Use the mask to extract the face mask region of interest
            masked_face = cv2.bitwise_and(face_mask_small, face_mask_small,
    mask=mask)
            # Use the inverse mask to get the remaining part of the image
            masked_frame = cv2.bitwise_and(frame_roi, frame_roi,
    mask=mask_inv)
        except cv2.error as e:
            print('Ignoring arithmentic exceptions: '+ str(e))

        # add the two images to get the final output
        frame[y:y+h, x:x+w] = cv2.add(masked_face, masked_frame)

    cv2.imshow('Face Detector', frame)

    c = cv2.waitKey(1)
    if c == 27:
        break

cap.release()
cv2.destroyAllWindows()
```

Under the hood

Just like before, we first load the face cascade classifier XML file. The face detection steps work as usual. We start the infinite loop and keep detecting the face in every frame. Once we know where the face is, we need to modify the coordinates a bit to make sure the mask fits properly. This manipulation process is subjective and depends on the mask in question. Different masks require different levels of adjustments to make it look more natural. We extract the region-of-interest from the input frame in the following line:

```
frame_roi = frame[y:y+h, x:x+w]
```

Now that we have the required region-of-interest, we need to overlay the mask on top of this. So we resize the input mask to make sure it fits in this region-of-interest. The input mask has a white background. So if we just overlay this on top of the region-of-interest, it will look unnatural because of the white background. We need to overlay only the skull-mask pixels; the remaining area should be transparent.

So, in the next step, we create a mask by thresholding the skull image. Since the background is white, we threshold the image so that any pixel with an intensity value greater than 180 becomes zero, and everything else becomes 255. As far as the frame region-of-interest is concerned, we need to black out everything in this mask region. We can do that by simply using the inverse of the mask we just created. Once we have the masked versions of the skull image and the input region-of-interest, we just add them up to get the final image.

Removing the alpha channel from the overlay image

Due to the use of overlay images, we should keep in mind that a layer might be built on black pixels, which will produce an undesired effect on the outcome of our code. Aiming to avoid that problem, the following code removes the alpha channel layer from your overlay images, and therefore allows us to obtain good results on the sample codes we have in this chapter:

```python
import numpy as np
import cv2

def remove_alpha_channel(source, background_color):
    source_img = cv2.cvtColor(source[:,:,:3], cv2.COLOR_BGR2GRAY)
    source_mask = source[:,:,3] * (1 / 255.0)
    bg_part = (255 * (1 / 255.0)) * (1.0 - source_mask)
    weight = (source_img * (1 / 255.0)) * (source_mask)
    dest = np.uint8(cv2.addWeighted(bg_part, 255.0, weight, 255.0, 0.0))
    return dest

orig_img = cv2.imread('./images/overlay_source.png', cv2.IMREAD_UNCHANGED)
dest_img = remove_alpha_channel(orig_img)
cv2.imwrite('images/overlay_dest.png', dest_img,
[cv2.IMWRITE_PNG_COMPRESSION])
```

Detecting eyes

Now that we understand how to detect faces, we can generalize the concept to detect other body parts too. It's important to understand that the Viola-Jones framework can be applied to any object. The accuracy and robustness will depend on the uniqueness of the object. For example, a human face has very unique characteristics, so it's easy to train our system to be robust. On the other hand, objects like towels, clothes or books are too generic, and there are no distinguishing characteristics as such, so it's more difficult to build a robust detector.

Let's see how to build an eye detector:

```python
import cv2
import numpy as np

face_cascade =
cv2.CascadeClassifier('./cascade_files/haarcascade_frontalface_alt.xml')
eye_cascade = cv2.CascadeClassifier('./cascade_files/haarcascade_eye.xml')
if face_cascade.empty():
  raise IOError('Unable to load the face cascade classifier xml file')

if eye_cascade.empty():
  raise IOError('Unable to load the eye cascade classifier xml file')

cap = cv2.VideoCapture(0)
ds_factor = 0.5

while True:
    ret, frame = cap.read()
    frame = cv2.resize(frame, None, fx=ds_factor, fy=ds_factor,
interpolation=cv2.INTER_AREA)
    gray = cv2.cvtColor(frame, cv2.COLOR_BGR2GRAY)

    faces = face_cascade.detectMultiScale(gray, scaleFactor=1.3,
minNeighbors=1)
    for (x,y,w,h) in faces:
        roi_gray = gray[y:y+h, x:x+w]
        roi_color = frame[y:y+h, x:x+w]
        eyes = eye_cascade.detectMultiScale(roi_gray)
        for (x_eye,y_eye,w_eye,h_eye) in eyes:
            center = (int(x_eye + 0.5*w_eye), int(y_eye + 0.5*h_eye))
            radius = int(0.3 * (w_eye + h_eye))
            color = (0, 255, 0)
            thickness = 3
            cv2.circle(roi_color, center, radius, color, thickness)

    cv2.imshow('Eye Detector', frame)

    c = cv2.waitKey(1)
    if c == 27:
        break

cap.release()
cv2.destroyAllWindows()
```

If you run this program, the output will look something like the following image:

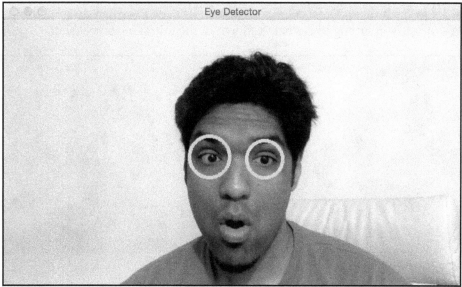

Afterthought

If you notice, this program looks very similar to the face detection program. Along with loading the face detection cascade classifier, we load the eye detection cascade classifier as well. Technically, we don't need to use the face detector. But we know that eyes are always on somebody's face. We use this information and search for eyes only in the relevant region of interest, that is, the face. We first detect the face, and then run the eye detector on this sub-image. This way, it's faster and more efficient.

Fun with eyes

Now that we know how to detect eyes in an image, let's see if we can do something fun with it. We can do something like what is shown in the following screenshot:

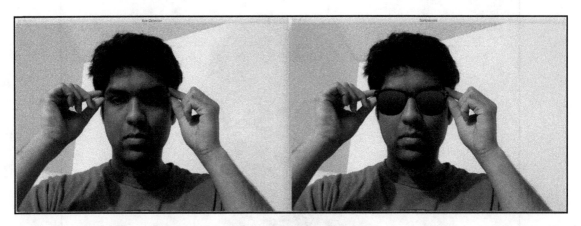

Let's look at the code to see how to do something like this:

```
import cv2
import numpy as np

face_cascade =
cv2.CascadeClassifier('./cascade_files/haarcascade_frontalface_alt.xml')
eye_cascade = cv2.CascadeClassifier('./cascade_files/haarcascade_eye.xml')

if face_cascade.empty():
  raise IOError('Unable to load the face cascade classifier xml file')
if eye_cascade.empty():
  raise IOError('Unable to load the eye cascade classifier xml file')

cap = cv2.VideoCapture(0)
sunglasses_img = cv2.imread('images/sunglasses.png')

while True:
    ret, frame = cap.read()
    frame = cv2.resize(frame, None, fx=0.5, fy=0.5,
interpolation=cv2.INTER_AREA)
    vh, vw = frame.shape[:2]
    vh, vw = int(vh), int(vw)

    gray = cv2.cvtColor(frame, cv2.COLOR_BGR2GRAY)
    faces = face_cascade.detectMultiScale(gray, scaleFactor=1.3,
minNeighbors=1)
```

```
    centers = []

for (x,y,w,h) in faces:
    roi_gray = gray[y:y+h, x:x+w]
    roi_color = frame[y:y+h, x:x+w]
    eyes = eye_cascade.detectMultiScale(roi_gray)
    for (x_eye,y_eye,w_eye,h_eye) in eyes:
        centers.append((x + int(x_eye + 0.5*w_eye), y + int(y_eye +
0.5*h_eye)))
    if len(centers) > 1: # if detects both eyes
        h, w = sunglasses_img.shape[:2]
        # Extract the region of interest from the image
        eye_distance = abs(centers[1][0] - centers[0][0])
        # Overlay sunglasses; the factor 2.12 is customizable depending on
the size of the face
        sunglasses_width = 2.12 * eye_distance
        scaling_factor = sunglasses_width / w
        print(scaling_factor, eye_distance)
        overlay_sunglasses = cv2.resize(sunglasses_img, None,
fx=scaling_factor, fy=scaling_factor, interpolation=cv2.INTER_AREA)

        x = centers[0][0] if centers[0][0] < centers[1][0] else
centers[1][0]
        # customizable X and Y locations; depends on the size of the face
        x -= int(0.26*overlay_sunglasses.shape[1])
        y += int(0.26*overlay_sunglasses.shape[0])
        h, w = overlay_sunglasses.shape[:2]
        h, w = int(h), int(w)
        frame_roi = frame[y:y+h, x:x+w]
        # Convert color image to grayscale and threshold it
        gray_overlay_sunglassess = cv2.cvtColor(overlay_sunglasses,
cv2.COLOR_BGR2GRAY)
        ret, mask = cv2.threshold(gray_overlay_sunglassess, 180, 255,
cv2.THRESH_BINARY_INV)

        # Create an inverse mask
        mask_inv = cv2.bitwise_not(mask)

        try:
            # Use the mask to extract the face mask region of interest
            masked_face = cv2.bitwise_and(overlay_sunglasses,
overlay_sunglasses, mask=mask)
            # Use the inverse mask to get the remaining part of the image
            masked_frame = cv2.bitwise_and(frame_roi, frame_roi,
mask=mask_inv)
        except cv2.error as e:
            print('Ignoring arithmentic exceptions: '+ str(e))
            #raise e
```

```
        # add the two images to get the final output
        frame[y:y+h, x:x+w] = cv2.add(masked_face, masked_frame)
    else:
        print('Eyes not detected')

    cv2.imshow('Eye Detector', frame)
    c = cv2.waitKey(1)
    if c == 27:
        break

cap.release()
cv2.destroyAllWindows()
```

Positioning the sunglasses

Just like we did earlier, we load the image and detect the eyes. Once we detect the eyes, we resize the sunglasses image to fit the current region of interest. To create the region of interest, we consider the distance between the eyes. We resize the image accordingly and then go ahead and create a mask. This is similar to what we did with the skull mask earlier. The positioning of the sunglasses on the face is subjective, so you will have to tinker with the weights if you want to use a different pair of sunglasses.

Detecting ears

Once more, through the use of Haar cascade classifier files, the code below will identify each ear, highlighting them once they are detected. As you can notice, two different classifiers are required as the coordinates for each ear will be inverted:

```
import cv2
import numpy as np

left_ear_cascade =
cv2.CascadeClassifier('./cascade_files/haarcascade_mcs_leftear.xml')
right_ear_cascade =
cv2.CascadeClassifier('./cascade_files/haarcascade_mcs_rightear.xml')

if left_ear_cascade.empty():
  raise IOError('Unable to load the left ear cascade classifier xml file')

if right_ear_cascade.empty():
  raise IOError('Unable to load the right ear cascade classifier xml file')

cap = cv2.VideoCapture(0)
```

```
scaling_factor = 0.5
while True:
  ret, frame = cap.read()
  frame = cv2.resize(frame, None, fx=scaling_factor, fy=scaling_factor,
interpolation=cv2.INTER_AREA)
  gray = cv2.cvtColor(frame, cv2.COLOR_BGR2GRAY)

  left_ear = left_ear_cascade.detectMultiScale(gray, scaleFactor=1.3,
minNeighbors=3)
  right_ear = right_ear_cascade.detectMultiScale(gray, scaleFactor=1.3,
minNeighbors=3)

  for (x,y,w,h) in left_ear:
    cv2.rectangle(frame, (x,y), (x+w,y+h), (0,255,0), 3)

  for (x,y,w,h) in right_ear:
    cv2.rectangle(frame, (x,y), (x+w,y+h), (255,0,0), 3)

  cv2.imshow('Ear Detector', frame)
  c = cv2.waitKey(1)
  if c == 27:
    break

cap.release()
cv2.destroyAllWindows()
```

If you run the preceding code on an image, you should see something like the following screenshot:

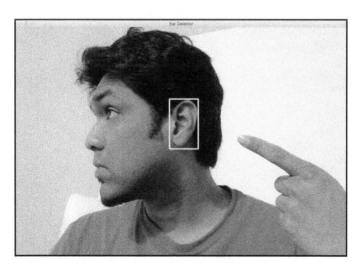

Detecting a mouth

This time, using Haar classifiers, we are going to extract a mouth position from the input video stream, and on the code below this code we are going to use those coordinates to place a mustache on the face:

```
import cv2
import numpy as np

mouth_cascade =
cv2.CascadeClassifier('./cascade_files/haarcascade_mcs_mouth.xml')
if mouth_cascade.empty():
  raise IOError('Unable to load the mouth cascade classifier xml file')

cap = cv2.VideoCapture(0)
ds_factor = 0.5

while True:
    ret, frame = cap.read()
    frame = cv2.resize(frame, None, fx=ds_factor, fy=ds_factor,
interpolation=cv2.INTER_AREA)
    gray = cv2.cvtColor(frame, cv2.COLOR_BGR2GRAY)

    mouth_rects = mouth_cascade.detectMultiScale(gray, scaleFactor=1.7,
minNeighbors=11)
    for (x,y,w,h) in mouth_rects:
        y = int(y - 0.15*h)
        cv2.rectangle(frame, (x,y), (x+w,y+h), (0,255,0), 3)
        break

    cv2.imshow('Mouth Detector', frame)

    c = cv2.waitKey(1)
    if c == 27:
        break

cap.release()
cv2.destroyAllWindows()
```

The following image shows what the output looks like:

It's time for a moustache

Let's overlay a moustache on top:

```
import cv2
import numpy as np

mouth_cascade =
cv2.CascadeClassifier('./cascade_files/haarcascade_mcs_mouth.xml')

moustache_mask = cv2.imread('./images/moustache.png')
h_mask, w_mask = moustache_mask.shape[:2]

if mouth_cascade.empty():
  raise IOError('Unable to load the mouth cascade classifier xml file')

cap = cv2.VideoCapture(0)
scaling_factor = 0.5

while True:
    ret, frame = cap.read()
    frame = cv2.resize(frame, None, fx=scaling_factor, fy=scaling_factor,
interpolation=cv2.INTER_AREA)
    gray = cv2.cvtColor(frame, cv2.COLOR_BGR2GRAY)
```

```
        mouth_rects = mouth_cascade.detectMultiScale(gray, 1.3, 5)
        if len(mouth_rects) > 0:
            (x,y,w,h) = mouth_rects[0]
            h, w = int(0.6*h), int(1.2*w)
            x -= int(0.05*w)
            y -= int(0.55*h)
            frame_roi = frame[y:y+h, x:x+w]
            moustache_mask_small = cv2.resize(moustache_mask, (w, h),
    interpolation=cv2.INTER_AREA)

            gray_mask = cv2.cvtColor(moustache_mask_small, cv2.COLOR_BGR2GRAY)
            ret, mask = cv2.threshold(gray_mask, 50, 255,
    cv2.THRESH_BINARY_INV)
            mask_inv = cv2.bitwise_not(mask)
            masked_mouth = cv2.bitwise_and(moustache_mask_small,
    moustache_mask_small, mask=mask)
            masked_frame = cv2.bitwise_and(frame_roi, frame_roi, mask=mask_inv)
            frame[y:y+h, x:x+w] = cv2.add(masked_mouth, masked_frame)

        cv2.imshow('Moustache', frame)
        c = cv2.waitKey(1)
        if c == 27:
            break

    cap.release()
    cv2.destroyAllWindows()
```

Here's what it looks like:

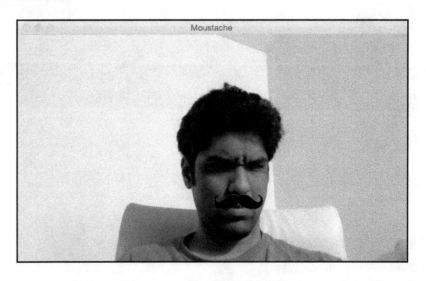

Detecting pupils

We are going to take a different approach here. Pupils are too generic to take the Haar cascade approach. We will also get a sense of how to detect things based on their shape. The following is what the output will look like:

Let's see how to build the pupil detector:

```
import math

import cv2

eye_cascade = cv2.CascadeClassifier('./cascade_files/haarcascade_eye.xml')
if eye_cascade.empty():
  raise IOError('Unable to load the eye cascade classifier xml file')

cap = cv2.VideoCapture(0)
ds_factor = 0.5
ret, frame = cap.read()
contours = []

while True:
  ret, frame = cap.read()
  frame = cv2.resize(frame, None, fx=ds_factor, fy=ds_factor,
interpolation=cv2.INTER_AREA)
  gray = cv2.cvtColor(frame, cv2.COLOR_BGR2GRAY)
```

```
    eyes = eye_cascade.detectMultiScale(gray, scaleFactor=1.3,
minNeighbors=1)
    for (x_eye, y_eye, w_eye, h_eye) in eyes:
        pupil_frame = gray[y_eye:y_eye + h_eye, x_eye:x_eye + w_eye]
        ret, thresh = cv2.threshold(pupil_frame, 80, 255, cv2.THRESH_BINARY)
        cv2.imshow("threshold", thresh)
        im2, contours, hierarchy = cv2.findContours(thresh, cv2.RETR_LIST,
cv2.CHAIN_APPROX_SIMPLE)
        print(contours)

        for contour in contours:
            area = cv2.contourArea(contour)
            rect = cv2.boundingRect(contour)
            x, y, w, h = rect
            radius = 0.15 * (w + h)

            area_condition = (100 <= area <= 200)
            symmetry_condition = (abs(1 - float(w)/float(h)) <= 0.2)
            fill_condition = (abs(1 - (area / (math.pi * math.pow(radius, 2.0))))
<= 0.4)
            cv2.circle(frame, (int(x_eye + x + radius), int(y_eye + y + radius)),
int(1.3 * radius), (0, 180, 0), -1)

    cv2.imshow('Pupil Detector', frame)
    c = cv2.waitKey(1)
    if c == 27:
        break
cap.release()
cv2.destroyAllWindows()
```

If you run this program, you will see the output as shown earlier.

Deconstructing the code

As we discussed earlier, we are not going to use Haar cascade to detect pupils. If we can't use a pre-trained classifier, then how are we going to detect the pupils? Well, we can use shape analysis to detect the pupils. We know that pupils are circular, so we can use this information to detect them in the image. We invert the input image and then convert it into a grayscale image as shown in the following line:

```
gray = cv2.cvtColor(img, cv2.COLOR_BGR2GRAY)
```

As we can see here, we can invert an image using the tilde operator. Inverting the image is helpful in our case because the pupil is black in color, and black corresponds to a low pixel value. We then threshold the image to make sure that there are only black and white pixels. Now, we have to find out the boundaries of all the shapes. OpenCV provides a nice function to achieve this, that is `findContours`. We will discuss more about this in the upcoming chapters. But for now, all we need to know is that this function returns the set of boundaries of all the shapes that are found in the image.

The next step is to identify the shape of the pupil and discard the rest. We will use certain properties of the circle to zero-in on this shape. Let's consider the width to height ratio of the bounding rectangle. If the shape is a circle, this ratio will be one. We can use the `boundingRect` function to obtain the coordinates of the bounding rectangle. Let's consider the area of this shape. If we roughly compute the radius of this shape and use the formula for the area of the circle, then it should be close to the area of this contour. We can use the `contourArea` function to compute the area of any contour in the image. So, we can use these conditions and filter out the shapes. After we do that, we are left with two pupils in the image. We can refine it further by limiting the search region to the face or the eyes. Since you know how to detect faces and eyes, you can give it a try and see if you can get it working for a live video stream.

 If you feel like playing with another kind of body detection, just go to the following link to find the difference classifiers: ;https://github.com/opencv/opencv/tree/master/data/haarcascades

Summary

In this chapter, we discussed Haar cascades and integral images. We understood how the face detection pipeline is built. We learned how to detect and track faces in a live video stream. We discussed how to use the face detection pipeline to detect various body parts, such as eyes, ears, nose, and mouth. We learned how to overlay masks on top on the input image using the results of body parts detection. We used the principles of shape analysis to detect the pupils.

In the next chapter, we are going to discuss feature detection and how it can be used to understand image content.

5
Extracting Features from an Image

In this chapter, we are going to learn how to detect salient points, also known as keypoints, in an image. We will discuss why these keypoints are important and how we can use them to understand image content. We will talk about different techniques that can be used to detect these keypoints, and understand how we can extract features from a given image.

By the end of this chapter, you will know the following:

- What are keypoints and why do we care about them?
- How to detect keypoints
- How to use keypoints for image content analysis
- The different techniques for detecting keypoints
- How to build a feature extractor

Why do we care about keypoints?

Image content analysis refers to the process of understanding the content of an image so that we can take some action based on that. Let's take a step back and talk about how humans do it. Our brain is an extremely powerful machine that can do complicated things very quickly. When we look at something, our brain automatically creates a footprint based on the *interesting* aspects of that image. We will discuss what interesting means as we progress through this chapter.

For now, an interesting aspect is something that's distinct in that region. If we call a point interesting, then there shouldn't be another point in its neighborhood that satisfies the constraints. Let's consider the following image:

Now, close your eyes and try to visualize this image. Do you see something specific? Can you recollect what's in the left half of the image? Not really! The reason for this is that the image doesn't have any interesting information. When our brain looks at something like this, there's nothing to make note of, so it tends to wander around! Let's take a look at the following image:

Now, close your eyes and try to visualize this image. You will see that the recollection is vivid and you remember a lot of details about this image. The reason for this is that there are a lot of interesting regions in the image. The human eye is more sensitive to high-frequency content then low-frequency content. This is the reason we tend to recollect the second image better than the first one. To further demonstrate this, let's look at the following image:

If you notice, your eye immediately went to the TV remote, even though it's not at the center of the image. We automatically tend to gravitate towards the interesting regions in the image because that is where all the information is. This is what our brain needs to store in order to recollect it later.

When we build object recognition systems, we need to detect these *interesting* regions to create a signature for the image. These interesting regions are characterized by keypoints. This is why keypoint detection is critical in many modern computer vision systems.

What are keypoints?

Now that we know that keypoints refer to the interesting regions in the image, let's dig a little deeper. What are keypoints made of? Where are these points? When we say *interesting*, it means that something is happening in that region. If the region is just uniform, then it's not very interesting. For example, corners are interesting because there is a sharp change in intensity in two different directions. Each corner is a unique point where two edges meet. If you look at the preceding images, you will see that the interesting regions are not completely made up of interesting content. If you look closely, we can still see plain regions within busy regions. For example, consider the following image:

If you look at the preceding object, the interior parts of the interesting regions are *uninteresting*:

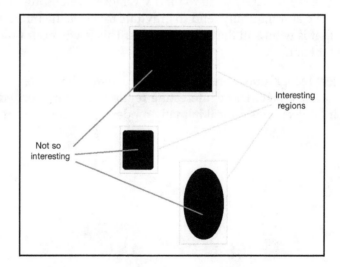

So, if we were to characterize this object, we would need to make sure that we picked the interesting points. Now, how do we define *interesting points*? Can we just say that anything that's not uninteresting can be an interesting point? Let's consider the following example:

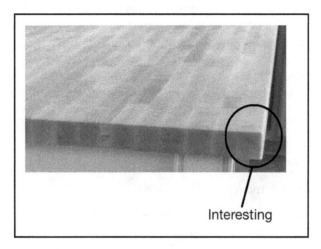

Interesting

Now, we can see that there is a lot of high-frequency content in this image along the edge. But we cannot call the whole edge *interesting*. It is important to understand that *interesting* doesn't necessarily refer to color or intensity values. It can be anything, as long as it is distinct. We need to isolate the points that are unique in their neighborhood. The points along the edge are not unique with respect to their neighbors. So, now that we know what we are looking for, how do we pick an interesting point?

What about the corner of the table? That's pretty interesting, right? It's unique with respect to its neighbors and we don't have anything like that in its vicinity. Now this point can be chosen as one of our keypoints. We take a bunch of these keypoints to characterize a particular image.

When we do image analysis, we need to convert the image into a numerical form before we deduce something. These keypoints are represented using a numerical form, and a combination of these keypoints is then used to create the image signature. We want this image signature to represent a given image in the best possible way.

Detecting the corners

Since we know that the corners are *interesting*, let's see how we can detect them. In computer vision, there is a popular corner detection technique called the **Harris Corner Detector**. We basically construct a 2x2 matrix based on partial derivatives of the grayscale image, and then analyze the eigenvalues obtained. Eigenvalues are a special set of scalars associated with a linear system of equations that provide segmented information about the image by a cluster of pixels that belong together. In this case, we use them to detect the corners. This is actually an oversimplification of the actual algorithm, but it covers the gist. So, if you want to understand the underlying mathematical details, you can look into the original paper by Harris and Stephens at http://www.bmva.org/bmvc/1988/avc-88-023.pdf. A corner point is a point where both the eigenvalues would have large values.

Let's consider the following image:

If you run the Harris Corner Detector on this image, you will see something like this:

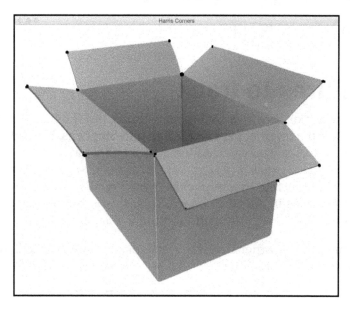

As you can see, all the black dots correspond to the corners in the image. You may notice that the corners at the bottom of the box are not detected. The reason for this is that the corners are not sharp enough. You can adjust the thresholds in the corner detector to identify these corners. The code to do this is as follows:

```
import cv2
import numpy as np

img = cv2.imread('./images/box.png')
gray = cv2.cvtColor(img,cv2.COLOR_BGR2GRAY)
gray = np.float32(gray)

# To detect only sharp corners
dst = cv2.cornerHarris(gray, blockSize=4, ksize=5, k=0.04)
# Result is dilated for marking the corners
dst = cv2.dilate(dst, None)

# Threshold for an optimal value, it may vary depending on the image
img[dst > 0.01*dst.max()] = [0,0,0]
cv2.imshow('Harris Corners(only sharp)',img)

# to detect soft corners
dst = cv2.cornerHarris(gray, blockSize=14, ksize=5, k=0.04)
dst = cv2.dilate(dst, None)
```

```
img[dst > 0.01*dst.max()] = [0,0,0]
cv2.imshow('Harris Corners(also soft)',img)

cv2.waitKey()
```

Good features to track

The Harris Corner Detector performs well in many cases, but it misses out on a few things. Around six years after the original paper by Harris and Stephens, Shi and Tomasi came up with a better corner detector. You can read the original paper at http://www.ai.mit.edu/courses/6.891/handouts/shi94good.pdf. J. Shi and C.Tomasi used a different scoring function to improve the overall quality. Using this method, we can find the N strongest corners in the given image. This is very useful when we don't want to use every single corner to extract information from the image.

If you apply the Shi-Tomasi Corner Detector to the image shown earlier, you will see something like this:

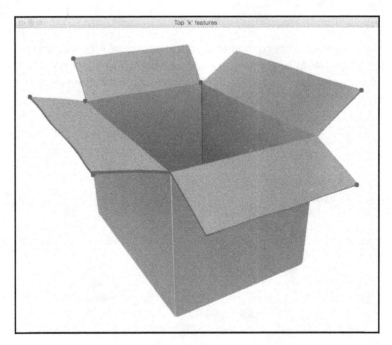

The following is the code:

```
import cv2
import numpy as np

img = cv2.imread('images/box.png')
gray = cv2.cvtColor(img,cv2.COLOR_BGR2GRAY)

corners = cv2.goodFeaturesToTrack(gray, maxCorners=7, qualityLevel=0.05,
minDistance=25)
corners = np.float32(corners)

for item in corners:
    x, y = item[0]
    cv2.circle(img, (x,y), 5, 255, -1)

cv2.imshow("Top 'k' features", img)
cv2.waitKey()
```

Scale-invariant feature transform (SIFT)

Even though corner features are *interesting*, they are not good enough to characterize the truly interesting parts. When we talk about image content analysis, we want the image signature to be invariant to things such as scale, rotation and illumination. Humans are very good at these things. Even if I show you an image of an apple upside down that's dimmed, you will still recognize it. If I show you a really enlarged version of that image, you will still recognize it. We want our image recognition systems to be able to do the same.

Let's consider the corner features. If you enlarge an image, a corner might stop being a corner, as follows:

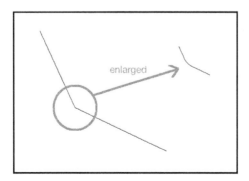

In the second case, the detector will not pick up this corner. And, since it was picked up in the original image, the second image will not be matched with the first one. It's basically the same image, but the corner features-based method will totally miss it. This means that a corner detector is not exactly scale-invariant. This is why we need a better method to characterize an image.

SIFT is one of the most popular algorithms in the entire field of computer vision. You can read David Lowe's original paper at http://www.cs.ubc.ca/~lowe/papers/ijcv04.pdf. We can use this algorithm to extract keypoints and build the corresponding feature descriptors. There is a lot of good documentation available online, so we will keep our discussion brief. To identify a potential keypoint, SIFT builds a pyramid by downsampling an image and taking the difference of Gaussian. This means that we run a Gaussian filter at each level and take the difference to build the successive levels in the pyramid. In order to see if the current point is a keypoint, it looks at the neighbors as well as the pixels at the same location in neighboring levels of the pyramid. If it's a maximum, then the current point is picked up as a keypoint. This ensures that we keep the keypoints scale-invariant.

Now that we know how SIFT achieves scale invariance, let's see how it achieves rotation invariance. Once we identify the keypoints, each keypoint is assigned an orientation. We take the neighborhood around each keypoint and compute the gradient magnitude and direction. This gives us a sense of the direction of that keypoint. If we have this information, we will be able to match this keypoint to the same point in another image even if it's rotated. Since we know the orientation, we will be able to normalize those keypoints before making the comparisons.

Once we have all this information, how do we quantify it? We need to convert it to a set of numbers so that we can do some kind of matching on it. To achieve this, we just take the 16x16 neighborhood around each keypoint, and divide it into 16 blocks of size 4x4. For each block, we compute the orientation histogram with eight bins. So, we have a vector of length eight associated with each block, which means that the neighborhood is represented by a vector of size 128 (8x16). This is the final keypoint descriptor that will be used. If we extract N keypoints from an image, then we will have N descriptors each of length 128. This array of N descriptors characterizes the given image.

Consider the following image:

If you extract the keypoint locations using SIFT, you will see something like the following, where the size of the circle indicates the strength of the keypoints, and the line inside the circle indicates the orientation:

Before we look at the code, it is important to know that SIFT is patented and it's not freely available for commercial use. The following is the code to do it:

```
import cv2
import numpy as np

input_image = cv2.imread('images/fishing_house.jpg')
gray_image = cv2.cvtColor(input_image, cv2.COLOR_BGR2GRAY)

# For version opencv < 3.0.0, use cv2.SIFT()
sift = cv2.xfeatures2d.SIFT_create()
keypoints = sift.detect(gray_image, None)

cv2.drawKeypoints(input_image, keypoints, input_image, \
  flags = cv2.DRAW_MATCHES_FLAGS_DRAW_RICH_KEYPOINTS)

cv2.imshow('SIFT features', input_image)
cv2.waitKey()
```

We can also compute the descriptors. OpenCV lets us do it separately, or we can combine the detection and computation parts in the same step by using the following:

```
keypoints, descriptors = sift.detectAndCompute(gray_image, None)
```

Speeded-up robust features (SURF)

Even though SIFT is nice and useful, it's computationally intensive. This means that it's slow and we will have a hard time implementing a real-time system if it uses SIFT. We need a system that's fast and has all the advantages of SIFT. If you remember, SIFT uses the Gaussian difference to build the pyramid, and this process is slow. So, to overcome this, SURF uses a simple box filter to approximate the Gaussian. The good thing is that this is really easy to compute and it's reasonably fast. There's a lot of documentation available online on SURF at http://opencv-python-tutroals.readthedocs.org/en/latest/py_tutorials/py_feature 2d/py_surf_intro/py_surf_intro.html?highlight=surf. So, you can go through it to see how they construct a descriptor. You can also refer to the original paper at http://www.vision.ee.ethz.ch/~surf/eccv06.pdf. It is important to know that SURF is also patented and it is not freely available for commercial use.

If you run the SURF keypoint detector on the earlier image, you will see something like this:

Here is the code:

```
import cv2
import numpy as np

input_image = cv2.imread('images/fishing_house.jpg')
gray_image = cv2.cvtColor(input_image, cv2.COLOR_BGR2GRAY)

# For version opencv < 3.0.0, use cv2.SURF()
surf = cv2.xfeatures2d.SURF_create()
# This threshold controls the number of keypoints
surf.setHessianThreshold(15000)

keypoints, descriptors = surf.detectAndCompute(gray_image, None)

cv2.drawKeypoints(input_image, keypoints, input_image, color=(0,255,0),\
flags=cv2.DRAW_MATCHES_FLAGS_DRAW_RICH_KEYPOINTS)

cv2.imshow('SURF features', input_image)
cv2.waitKey()
```

Features from accelerated segment test (FAST)

Even though SURF is faster than SIFT, it's just not fast enough for a real-time system, especially when there are resource constraints. When you are building a real-time application on a mobile device, you won't have the luxury of using SURF to do computations in real time. We need something that's really fast and computationally inexpensive. Hence, Rosten and Drummond came up with FAST. As the name indicates, it's really fast!

Instead of going through all the expensive calculations, they came up with a high-speed test to quickly determine if the current point is a potential keypoint. We need to note that FAST is just for keypoint detection. Once keypoints are detected, we need to use SIFT or SURF to compute the descriptors. Consider the following image:

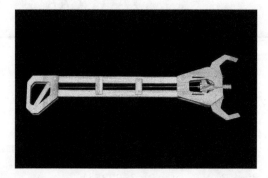

If we run the FAST keypoint detector on this image, you will see something like this:

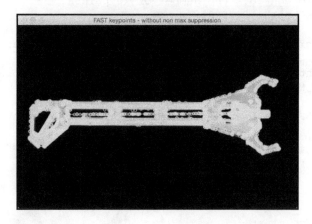

If we clean it up and suppress the unimportant keypoints, it will look like this:

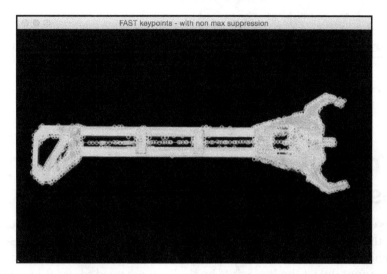

The following is the code for this:

```
import cv2
import numpy as np

input_image = cv2.imread('images/tool.png')
gray_image = cv2.cvtColor(input_image, cv2.COLOR_BGR2GRAY)

# Version under opencv 3.0.0 cv2.FastFeatureDetector()
fast = cv2.FastFeatureDetector_create()

# Detect keypoints
keypoints = fast.detect(gray_image, None)
print("Number of keypoints with non max suppression:", len(keypoints))


# Draw keypoints on top of the input image
img_keypoints_with_nonmax=input_image.copy()
cv2.drawKeypoints(input_image, keypoints, img_keypoints_with_nonmax,
color=(0,255,0), \ flags=cv2.DRAW_MATCHES_FLAGS_DRAW_RICH_KEYPOINTS)
cv2.imshow('FAST keypoints - with non max suppression',
img_keypoints_with_nonmax)

# Disable nonmaxSuppression
fast.setNonmaxSuppression(False)
# Detect keypoints again
keypoints = fast.detect(gray_image, None)
```

```
print("Total Keypoints without nonmaxSuppression:", len(keypoints))

# Draw keypoints on top of the input image
img_keypoints_without_nonmax=input_image.copy()
cv2.drawKeypoints(input_image, keypoints, img_keypoints_without_nonmax,
color=(0,255,0), \ flags=cv2.DRAW_MATCHES_FLAGS_DRAW_RICH_KEYPOINTS)
cv2.imshow('FAST keypoints - without non max suppression',
img_keypoints_without_nonmax)
cv2.waitKey()
```

Binary robust independent elementary features (BRIEF)

Even though we have FAST to quickly detect the keypoints, we still have to use SIFT or SURF to compute the descriptors. We need a way to quickly compute the descriptors as well. This is where BRIEF comes into the picture. BRIEF is a method for extracting feature descriptors. It cannot detect the keypoints by itself, so we need to use it in conjunction with a keypoint detector. The good thing about BRIEF is that it's compact and fast.

Consider the following image:

BRIEF takes the list of input keypoints and outputs an updated list. So, if you run BRIEF on this image, you will see something like this:

The following is the code:

```
import cv2
import numpy as np

input_image = cv2.imread('images/house.jpg')
gray_image = cv2.cvtColor(input_image, cv2.COLOR_BGR2GRAY)

# Initiate FAST detector
fast = cv2.FastFeatureDetector_create()

# Initiate BRIEF extractor, before opencv 3.0.0 use
cv2.DescriptorExtractor_create("BRIEF")
brief = cv2.xfeatures2d.BriefDescriptorExtractor_create()

# find the keypoints with STAR
keypoints = fast.detect(gray_image, None)

# compute the descriptors with BRIEF
keypoints, descriptors = brief.compute(gray_image, keypoints)
```

```
cv2.drawKeypoints(input_image, keypoints, input_image, color=(0,255,0))
cv2.imshow('BRIEF keypoints', input_image)
cv2.waitKey()
```

Oriented FAST and Rotated BRIEF (ORB)

So, now we have arrived at the best combination out of all the combinations that we have discussed so far. This algorithm came out of the OpenCV Labs. It's fast, robust, and open source! The SIFT and SURF algorithms are both patented and you can't use them for commercial purposes; this is why ORB is good in many ways.

If you run the ORB keypoint extractor on one of the images shown earlier, you will see something like the following:

Here is the code:

```
import cv2
import numpy as np

input_image = cv2.imread('images/fishing_house.jpg')
gray_image = cv2.cvtColor(input_image, cv2.COLOR_BGR2GRAY)

# Initiate ORB object, before opencv 3.0.0 use cv2.ORB()
orb = cv2.ORB_create()
```

```
# find the keypoints with ORB
keypoints = orb.detect(gray_image, None)

# compute the descriptors with ORB
keypoints, descriptors = orb.compute(gray_image, keypoints)

# draw only the location of the keypoints without size or orientation
cv2.drawKeypoints(input_image, keypoints, input_image, color=(0,255,0))

cv2.imshow('ORB keypoints', input_image)
cv2.waitKey()
```

Summary

In this chapter, we learned about the importance of keypoints and why we need them. We discussed various algorithms for detecting keypoints and computing feature descriptors. We will be using these algorithms in all the subsequent chapters in various contexts. The concept of keypoints is central to computer vision, and plays an important role in many modern systems.

In the next chapter, we are going to discuss how to stitch multiple images of the same scene together to create a panoramic image.

6
Seam Carving

In this chapter, we are going to learn about content-aware image resizing, which is also known as **seam carving**. We will discuss how to detect *interesting* parts in an image and how to use that information to resize a given image without deteriorating the quality of those interesting elements.

By the end of this chapter, you will know:

- What content awareness is
- How to quantify and identify interesting parts in an image
- How to use dynamic programming for image content analysis
- How to increase and decrease the width of an image without deteriorating the interesting regions while keeping the height constant
- How to make an object disappear from an image

Why do we care about seam carving?

Before we start our discussion about seam carving, we need to understand why it is needed in the first place. Why should we care about the image content? Why can't we just resize the given image and move on with our lives? Well, to answer those questions, let's consider the following image:

Now, let's say we want to reduce the width of this image while keeping the height constant. If we do that, it will look something like this:

As you can see, the ducks in the image look skewed, and there's degradation in the overall quality of the image. Intuitively speaking, we can say that the ducks are the interesting parts in the image. So, when we resize it, we want the ducks to be intact. This is where seam carving comes into the picture. Using seam carving, we can detect these interesting regions and make sure they don't get degraded.

How does it work?

We have been talking about image resizing and how we should consider the image's content when we resize it. So why on earth is it called seam carving? It should just be called content-aware image resizing, right? Well, there are many different terms that are used to describe this process, such as image re-targeting, liquid scaling, seam carving, and so on. It's called seam carving because of the way we resize the image. The algorithm was proposed by Shai Avidan and Ariel Shamir. You can refer to the original paper at `http://dl.acm.org/citation.cfm?id=1276390`.

We know that the goal is to resize the given image and keep the interesting content intact. So, we do that by finding the paths of least importance in the image. These paths are called seams. Once we find these seams, we remove or stretch them from the image to obtain a re-scaled image. This process of removing or stretching, or carving, will eventually result in a resized image. This is the reason we call it seam carving. Consider the following image:

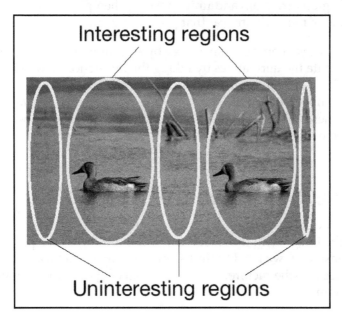

In the preceding image, we can see how to roughly divide the image into interesting and uninteresting parts. We need to make sure that our algorithm detects these uninteresting parts and works with them. Let's consider the image of the ducks and the constraints we have to deal with. We want to keep the height constant and reduce the width. This means that we need to find vertical seams in the image and remove them. These seams start at the top and end at the bottom (or vice versa). If we were dealing with vertical resizing, then the seams would start on the left-hand side and end on the right. A vertical seam is just a bunch of connected pixels starting in the first row and ending in the last row of the image.

How do we define interesting?

Before we start computing the seams, we need to find out what metric we will be using to compute them. We need a way to assign *importance* to each pixel so that we can identify the paths that are least important. In computer vision terminology, we say that we need to assign an *energy* value to each pixel so that we can find the path of minimum energy. Coming up with a good way to assign the energy value is very important because it will affect the quality of the output.

One of the metrics that we can use is the value of the derivative at each point. This is a good indicator of the level of activity in that neighborhood. If there is some activity, then the pixel values will change rapidly, hence the value of the derivative at that point will be high. On the other hand, if regions are plain and uninteresting, then pixel values won't change as rapidly, so the value of the derivative at that point in the grayscale image will be low.

For each pixel location, we compute the energy by summing up the x and y derivatives at that point. We compute the derivatives by taking the difference between the current pixel and its neighbors. If you recall, we did something similar to this when we were doing edge detection using the **sobel filter** in `Chapter 2`, *Detecting Edges and Applying Image Filters*. Once we compute these values, we store them in a matrix called the energy matrix, which will be used to define the seams.

How do we compute the seams?

Now that we have the energy matrix, we are ready to compute the seams. We need to find the path through the image with the least energy. Computing all the possible paths is prohibitively expensive, so we need to find a smarter way to do this. This is where dynamic programming comes into the picture. In fact, seam carving is a direct application of dynamic programming.

We need to start with each pixel in the first row and find our way to the last row. In order to find the path of least energy, we compute and store the best paths to each pixel in a table. Once we've constructed this table, the path to a particular pixel can be found by backtracking through the rows in that table.

For each pixel in the current row, we calculate the energy of three possible pixel locations in the next row that we can move to; that is, bottom left, bottom, and bottom right. We keep repeating this process until we reach the bottom. Once we reach the bottom, we take the one with the least cumulative value and backtrack our way to the top. This will give us the path of least energy. Every time we remove a seam, the width of the image decreases by one pixel. So, we need to keep removing these seams until we arrive at the desired image size.

First, we will provide a set of functions to compute the energy within the image, locate its seams, and draw them. These functions are going to be used along every preceding code sample, and it could be included as a library in any of your customizations:

```python
# Draw vertical seam on top of the image
def overlay_vertical_seam(img, seam):
    img_seam_overlay = np.copy(img)

    # Extract the list of points from the seam
    x_coords, y_coords = np.transpose([(i,int(j)) for i,j in
enumerate(seam)])

    # Draw a green line on the image using the list of points
    img_seam_overlay[x_coords, y_coords] = (0,255,0)
    return img_seam_overlay

# Compute the energy matrix from the input image
def compute_energy_matrix(img):
    gray = cv2.cvtColor(img, cv2.COLOR_BGR2GRAY)

    # Compute X derivative of the image
    sobel_x = cv2.Sobel(gray,cv2.CV_64F, 1, 0, ksize=3)

    # Compute Y derivative of the image
    sobel_y = cv2.Sobel(gray,cv2.CV_64F, 0, 1, ksize=3)

    abs_sobel_x = cv2.convertScaleAbs(sobel_x)
    abs_sobel_y = cv2.convertScaleAbs(sobel_y)

    # Return weighted summation of the two images i.e. 0.5*X + 0.5*Y
    return cv2.addWeighted(abs_sobel_x, 0.5, abs_sobel_y, 0.5, 0)

# Find vertical seam in the input image
def find_vertical_seam(img, energy):
```

```
    rows, cols = img.shape[:2]

    # Initialize the seam vector with 0 for each element
    seam = np.zeros(img.shape[0])

    # Initialize distance and edge matrices
    dist_to = np.zeros(img.shape[:2]) + float('inf')
    dist_to[0,:] = np.zeros(img.shape[1])
    edge_to = np.zeros(img.shape[:2])

    # Dynamic programming; iterate using double loop and compute the paths
efficiently
    for row in range(rows-1):
        for col in range(cols):
            if col != 0 and dist_to[row+1, col-1] > dist_to[row, col] +
energy[row+1, col-1]:
                dist_to[row+1, col-1] = dist_to[row, col] + energy[row+1,
col-1]
                edge_to[row+1, col-1] = 1

            if dist_to[row+1, col] > dist_to[row, col] + energy[row+1,
col]:
                dist_to[row+1, col] = dist_to[row, col] + energy[row+1,
col]
                edge_to[row+1, col] = 0

            if col != cols-1 and \
                dist_to[row+1, col+1] > dist_to[row, col] + energy[row+1,
col+1]:
                    dist_to[row+1, col+1] = dist_to[row, col] +
energy[row+1, col+1]
                    edge_to[row+1, col+1] = -1

    # Retracing the path
    # Returns the indices of the minimum values along X axis.
    seam[rows-1] = np.argmin(dist_to[rows-1, :])
    for i in (x for x in reversed(range(rows)) if x > 0):
        seam[i-1] = seam[i] + edge_to[i, int(seam[i])]

    return seam
```

Let's consider our image of ducks again. If we compute the first 30 seams, it will look something like this:

These green lines indicate the paths of least importance. As we can see here, they carefully go around the ducks to make sure that the interesting regions are not touched. In the upper half of the image, the seams go around the twigs so that the quality is preserved. Technically speaking, the twigs are also interesting. If we continue and remove the first 100 seams, it will look something like this:

Now, compare this with the naively resized image. Doesn't it look better? The ducks look nicer in this version.

Let's take a look at the code and see how to do it:

```
import sys
import cv2
import numpy as np

# Remove the input vertical seam from the image
def remove_vertical_seam(img, seam):
    rows, cols = img.shape[:2]

    # To delete a point, move every point after it one step towards the
left
    for row in range(rows):
        for col in range(int(seam[row]), cols-1):
            img[row, col] = img[row, col+1]

    # Discard the last column to create the final output image
    img = img[:, 0:cols-1]
    return img

if __name__=='__main__':
    # Make sure the size of the input image is reasonable.
    # Large images take a lot of time to be processed.
    # Recommended size is 640x480.
    img_input = cv2.imread(sys.argv[1])

    # Use a small number to get started. Once you get an
    # idea of the processing time, you can use a bigger number.
    # To get started, you can set it to 20.
    num_seams = int(sys.argv[2])

    img = np.copy(img_input)
    img_overlay_seam = np.copy(img_input)
    energy = compute_energy_matrix(img)

    for i in range(num_seams):
        seam = find_vertical_seam(img, energy)
        img_overlay_seam = overlay_vertical_seam(img_overlay_seam, seam)
        img = remove_vertical_seam(img, seam)
        energy = compute_energy_matrix(img)
        print('Number of seams removed = ', i+1)

    cv2.imshow('Input', img_input)
    cv2.imshow('Seams', img_overlay_seam)
    cv2.imshow('Output', img)
    cv2.waitKey()
```

We use `remove_vertical_seam` to remove vertical seams from the original image, reducing the width of the image but keeping the interesting parts intact.

Can we expand an image?

We know that we can use seam carving to reduce the width of an image without deteriorating the interesting regions. So, naturally, we need to ask ourselves if we can expand an image without deteriorating the interesting regions. As it turns out, we can do it using the same logic. When we compute the seams, we just need to add a column instead of deleting one.

If we expand the image of the ducks naively, it will look something like this:

If we do it in a smarter way—that is, by using seam carving—it will look something like this:

As you can see, the width of the image has increased and the ducks don't look stretched. The following is the code to do it:

```python
import sys
import cv2
import numpy as np

# Add a vertical seam to the image
def add_vertical_seam(img, seam, num_iter):
    seam = seam + num_iter
    rows, cols = img.shape[:2]
    zero_col_mat = np.zeros((rows,1,3), dtype=np.uint8)
    img_extended = np.hstack((img, zero_col_mat))

    for row in range(rows):
        for col in range(cols, int(seam[row]), -1):
            img_extended[row, col] = img[row, col-1]

            # To insert a value between two columns, take the average
            # value of the neighbors. It looks smooth this way and we
            # can avoid unwanted artifacts.
            for i in range(3):
                v1 = img_extended[row, int(seam[row])-1, i]
                v2 = img_extended[row, int(seam[row])+1, i]
                img_extended[row, int(seam[row]), i] = (int(v1)+int(v2))/2

    return img_extended

if __name__=='__main__':
    img_input = cv2.imread(sys.argv[1])
    num_seams = int(sys.argv[2])
    img = np.copy(img_input)
    img_output = np.copy(img_input)
    img_overlay_seam = np.copy(img_input)
    energy = compute_energy_matrix(img) # Same than previous code sample

    for i in range(num_seams):
        seam = find_vertical_seam(img, energy) # Same than previous code sample
        img_overlay_seam = overlay_vertical_seam(img_overlay_seam, seam)
        img = remove_vertical_seam(img, seam) # Same than previous code sample
        img_output = add_vertical_seam(img_output, seam, i)
        energy = compute_energy_matrix(img)
        print('Number of seams added =', i+1)

    cv2.imshow('Input', img_input)
```

```
cv2.imshow('Seams', img_overlay_seam)
cv2.imshow('Output', img_output)
cv2.waitKey()
```

In this case, we added an extra function, `add_vertical_seam`, to the code. We use it to add vertical seams so that the image looks natural, adding seams to the image aiming to increase the width of it without modifying the original proportions of the *interesting* areas.

Can we remove an object completely?

This is perhaps the most interesting application of seam carving. We can make an object completely disappear from an image. Let's consider the following image:

Enclose the region to remove using your mouse:

After you remove the chair on the right, it will look something like this:

It's as if the chair never existed! Before we look at the code, it's important to know that this takes a while to run. So, just wait for a couple of minutes to get an idea of the processing time. You can adjust the input image size accordingly! Let's take a look at the code:

```python
import sys
import cv2
import numpy as np

# Draw rectangle on top of the input image
def draw_rectangle(event, x, y, flags, params):
    global x_init, y_init, drawing, top_left_pt, bottom_right_pt, img_orig

    # Detecting a mouse click
    if event == cv2.EVENT_LBUTTONDOWN:
        drawing = True
        x_init, y_init = x, y

    # Detecting mouse movement
    elif event == cv2.EVENT_MOUSEMOVE:
        if drawing:
            top_left_pt, bottom_right_pt = (x_init,y_init), (x,y)
            img[y_init:y, x_init:x] = 255 - img_orig[y_init:y, x_init:x]
            cv2.rectangle(img, top_left_pt, bottom_right_pt, (0,255,0), 2)

    # Detecting the mouse button up event
    elif event == cv2.EVENT_LBUTTONUP:
        drawing = False
        top_left_pt, bottom_right_pt = (x_init,y_init), (x,y)

        # Create the "negative" film effect for the selected
```

```
    # region
    img[y_init:y, x_init:x] = 255 - img[y_init:y, x_init:x]

    # Draw rectangle around the selected region
    cv2.rectangle(img, top_left_pt, bottom_right_pt, (0,255,0), 2)
    rect_final = (x_init, y_init, x-x_init, y-y_init)

    # Remove the object in the selected region
    remove_object(img_orig, rect_final)

# Computing the energy matrix using modified algorithm
def compute_energy_matrix_modified(img, rect_roi):
    # Compute weighted summation i.e. 0.5*X + 0.5*Y
    energy_matrix = compute_energy_matrix(img)
    x,y,w,h = rect_roi

    # We want the seams to pass through this region, so make sure the
energy values in this region are set to 0
    energy_matrix[y:y+h, x:x+w] = 0

    return energy_matrix

# Remove the object from the input region of interest
def remove_object(img, rect_roi):
    num_seams = rect_roi[2] + 10
    energy = compute_energy_matrix_modified(img, rect_roi)

    # Start a loop and rsemove one seam at a time
    for i in range(num_seams):
        # Find the vertical seam that can be removed
        seam = find_vertical_seam(img, energy)

        # Remove that vertical seam
        img = remove_vertical_seam(img, seam)
        x,y,w,h = rect_roi

        # Compute energy matrix after removing the seam
        energy = compute_energy_matrix_modified(img, (x,y,w-i,h))
        print('Number of seams removed =', i+1)

    img_output = np.copy(img)

    # Fill up the region with surrounding values so that the size
    # of the image remains unchanged
    for i in range(num_seams):
        seam = find_vertical_seam(img, energy)
        img = remove_vertical_seam(img, seam)
        img_output = add_vertical_seam(img_output, seam, i)
```

```
        energy = compute_energy_matrix(img)
        print('Number of seams added =', i+1)

    cv2.imshow('Input', img_input)
    cv2.imshow('Output', img_output)
    cv2.waitKey()

if __name__=='__main__':
    img_input = cv2.imread(sys.argv[1])
    drawing = False
    img = np.copy(img_input)
    img_orig = np.copy(img_input)

    cv2.namedWindow('Input')
    cv2.setMouseCallback('Input', draw_rectangle)
    print('Draw a rectangle with the mouse over the object to be removed')
    while True:
        cv2.imshow('Input', img)
        c = cv2.waitKey(10)
        if c == 27:
            break

    cv2.destroyAllWindows()
```

How did we do it?

The basic logic remains the same here. We are using seam carving to remove an object. Once we select the region of interest, we make all the seams pass through this region. We do this by manipulating the energy matrix after every iteration. We have added a new function called `compute_energy_matrix_modified` to achieve this. Once we compute the energy matrix, we assign a value of zero to this region of interest. This way, we force all the seams to pass through this area. After we remove all the seams related to this region, we keep adding the seams until we expand the image to its original width.

Summary

In this chapter, we learned about content-aware image resizing. We discussed how to quantify interesting and uninteresting regions in an image. We learned how to compute seams in an image and how to use dynamic programming to do it efficiently. We discussed how to use seam carving to reduce the width of an image, and how we can use the same logic to expand an image. We also learned how to remove an object from an image completely.

In the next chapter, we are going to discuss how to do shape analysis and image segmentation. We will see how to use those principles to find the exact boundaries of an object of interest in an image.

7
Detecting Shapes and Segmenting an Image

In this chapter, we are going to learn about shape analysis and image segmentation. We will learn how to recognize shapes and estimate the exact boundaries. We will discuss how to segment an image into its constituent parts using various methods. We will learn how to separate the foreground from the background as well.

By the end of this chapter, you will know:

- What is contour analysis and shape matching
- How to match shapes
- What is image segmentation
- How to segment an image into its constituent parts
- How to separate the foreground from the background
- How to use various techniques to segment an image

Contour analysis and shape matching

Contour analysis is a very useful tool in the field of computer vision. We deal with a lot of shapes in the real world, and contour analysis helps in analyzing those shapes using various algorithms. When we convert an image to grayscale and threshold it, we are left with a bunch of lines and contours. Once we understand the properties of different shapes, we will be able to extract detailed information from an image.

Let's say we want to identify the boomerang shape in the following image:

In order to do that, we first need to know what a regular boomerang looks like:

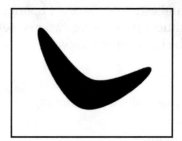

Now, using the preceding image as a reference, can we identify what shape in our original image corresponds to a boomerang? If you notice, we cannot use a simple correlation-based approach because the shapes are all distorted. This means that an approach where we look for an exact match will hardly work! We need to understand the features of the shape and match corresponding features to identify the boomerang shape. OpenCV provides several shape matcher utilities that we can use to achieve this. If you want to know more, go to `https://docs.opencv.org/3.3.0/dc/dc3/tutorial_py_matcher.html` for more information.

The matching is based on the concept of **Hu** moment, which in turn is related to image moments. You can refer to the following paper to learn more about moments: `http://zoi.utia.cas.cz/files/chapter_moments_color1.pdf`. The concept of *image moments* basically refers to the weighted and power-raised summation of the pixels within a shape.

$$I = \sum_{i=0}^{N} w_i p_i^k$$

In the preceding equation, p refers to the pixels inside the contour, w refers to the weights, N refers to the number of points inside the contour, k refers to the power, and I refers to the moment. Depending on the values we choose for w and k, we can extract different characteristics from that contour.

Perhaps the simplest example is to compute the area of the contour. To do this, we need to count the number of pixels within that region. So mathematically speaking, in the weighted and power-raised summation form, we just need to set w to one and k to zero. This will give us the area of the contour. Depending on how we compute these moments, they will help us in understanding these different shapes. This also gives rise to some interesting properties that help us in determining the shape-similarity metric.

If we match the shapes, you will see something like this:

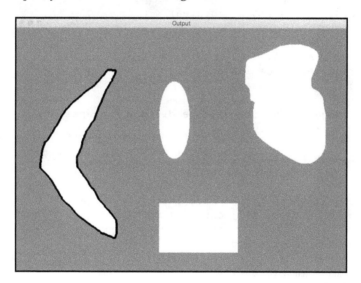

Let's take a look at the code to do this:

```
import cv2
import numpy as np

# Extract all the contours from the image
def get_all_contours(img):
    ref_gray = cv2.cvtColor(img, cv2.COLOR_BGR2GRAY)
    ret, thresh = cv2.threshold(ref_gray, 127, 255, 0)
```

```
        # Find all the contours in the thresholded image. The values
        # for the second and third parameters are restricted to a
        # certain number of possible values.
        im2, contours, hierarchy = cv2.findContours(thresh.copy(),
cv2.RETR_LIST, \
            cv2.CHAIN_APPROX_SIMPLE )
        return contours

# Extract reference contour from the image
def get_ref_contour(img):
    contours = get_all_contours(img)

    # Extract the relevant contour based on area ratio. We use the
    # area ratio because the main image boundary contour is
    # extracted as well and we don't want that. This area ratio
    # threshold will ensure that we only take the contour inside the image.
    for contour in contours:
        area = cv2.contourArea(contour)
        img_area = img.shape[0] * img.shape[1]
        if 0.05 < area/float(img_area) < 0.8:
            return contour

if __name__=='__main__':
    # Boomerang reference image
    img1 = cv2.imread(sys.argv[1])

    # Input image containing all the different shapes
    img2 = cv2.imread(sys.argv[2])

    # Extract the reference contour
    ref_contour = get_ref_contour(img1)

    # Extract all the contours from the input image
    input_contours = get_all_contours(img2)

        closest_contour = None
    min_dist = None
    contour_img = img2.copy()
    cv2.drawContours(contour_img, input_contours, -1, color=(0,0,0),
thickness=3)
    cv2.imshow('Contours', contour_img)
    # Finding the closest contour
    for contour in input_contours:
        # Matching the shapes and taking the closest one using
        # Comparison method CV_CONTOURS_MATCH_I3 (second argument)
        ret = cv2.matchShapes(ref_contour, contour, 3, 0.0)
        print("Contour %d matchs in %f" % (i, ret))
        if min_dist is None or ret < min_dist:
```

```
        min_dist = ret
        closest_contour = contour

    cv2.drawContours(img2, [closest_contour], 0 , color=(0,0,0),
thickness=3)
    cv2.imshow('Best Matching', img2)
    cv2.waitKey()
```

The use of the matchShapes method is possibly different from Hu invariants (CV_CONTOUR_MATCH_I1, 2, 3), where each method might produce different best-matched shapes due to the size, orientation, or rotation of the contours. To learn more, you can check the official documentation at https://docs.opencv.org/3.3.0/d3/dc0/group__imgproc__shape.html.

Approximating a contour

A lot of contours that we encounter in real life are noisy. This means that the contours don't look smooth, and hence our analysis takes a hit. So, how do we deal with this? One way to go about this would be to get all the points on the contour and then approximate it with a smooth polygon.

Let's consider the boomerang image again. If you approximate the contours using various thresholds, you will see the contours changing their shapes. Let's start with a factor of 0.05:

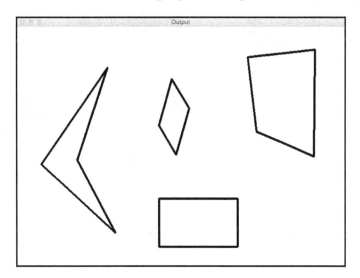

If you reduce this factor, the contours will get smoother. Let's make it 0.01:

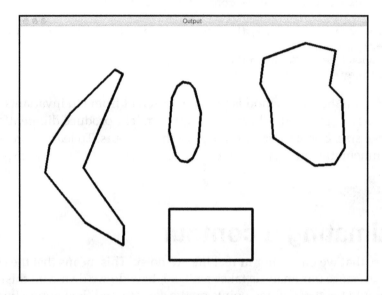

If you make it really small, say 0.00001, then it will look like the original image:

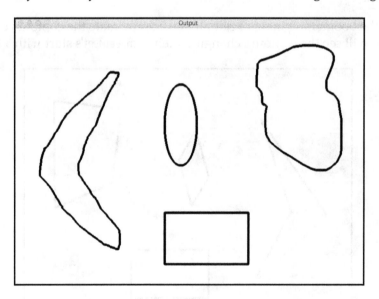

The following code represents how to convert those contours into approximate smoothing of polygons:

```
import sys
import cv2
import numpy as np

if __name__=='__main__':
    # Input image containing all the different shapes
    img1 = cv2.imread(sys.argv[1])
    # Extract all the contours from the input image
    input_contours = get_all_contours(img1)

    contour_img = img1.copy()
    smoothen_contours = []
    factor = 0.05

    # Finding the closest contour
    for contour in input_contours:
        epsilon = factor * cv2.arcLength(contour, True)
        smoothen_contours.append(cv2.approxPolyDP(contour, epsilon, True))

    cv2.drawContours(contour_img, smoothen_contours, -1, color=(0,0,0),
thickness=3)
    cv2.imshow('Contours', contour_img)
    cv2.waitKey()
```

Identifying a pizza with a slice taken out

The title might be slightly misleading, because we will not be talking about pizza slices. But let's say you are in a situation where you have an image containing different types of pizzas with different shapes. Now, somebody has taken a slice out of one of those pizzas. How would we automatically identify this?

We cannot take the approach we took earlier because we don't know what the shape looks like, so we don't have any template. We are not even sure what shape we are looking for, so we cannot build a template based on any prior information. All we know is the fact that a slice has been taken from one of the pizzas. Let's consider the following image:

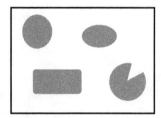

It's not exactly a real image, but you get the idea. You know what shape we are talking about. Since we don't know what we are looking for, we need to use some of the properties of these shapes to identify the sliced pizza. If you notice, all the other shapes are nicely closed; that is, you can take any two points within those shapes and draw a line between them, and that line will always lie within that shape. These kinds of shapes are called **convex shapes**.

If you look at the sliced pizza shape, we can choose two points such that the line between them goes outside the shape, as shown in the following figure:

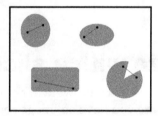

So, all we need to do is detect the non-convex shape in the image and we'll be done. Let's go ahead and do that:

```python
import sys
import cv2
import numpy as np

if __name__=='__main__':
    img = cv2.imread(sys.argv[1])

    # Iterate over the extracted contours
    # Using previous get_all_contours() method
    for contour in get_all_contours(img):
```

```
    # Extract convex hull from the contour
    hull = cv2.convexHull(contour, returnPoints=False)

    # Extract convexity defects from the above hull
    # Being a convexity defect the cavities in the hull segments
    defects = cv2.convexityDefects(contour, hull)

    if defects is None:
        continue

    # Draw lines and circles to show the defects
    for i in range(defects.shape[0]):
        start_defect, end_defect, far_defect, _ = defects[i,0]
        start = tuple(contour[start_defect][0])
        end = tuple(contour[end_defect][0])
        far = tuple(contour[far_defect][0])
        cv2.circle(img, far, 5, [128,0,0], -1)
        cv2.drawContours(img, [contour], -1, (0,0,0), 3)

cv2.imshow('Convexity defects',img)
cv2.waitKey(0)
cv2.destroyAllWindows()
```

To learn more about how `convexityDefects` works, you can go to `https://docs.opencv.org/2.4/modules/imgproc/doc/structural_analysis_and_shape_descriptors.html#convexitydefects`.

If you run the preceding code, you will see something like this:

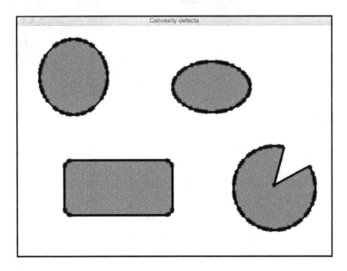

Wait a minute, what happened here? It looks so cluttered. Did we do something wrong? As it turns out, the curves are not really smooth. If you observe closely, there are tiny ridges everywhere along the curves. So, if you just run your convexity detector, it's not going to work.

This is where contour approximation comes in really handy. Once we've detected the contours, we need to smoothen them so that the ridges do not affect them. Let's go ahead and do that:

```
factor = 0.01
epsilon = factor * cv2.arcLength(contour, True)
contour = cv2.approxPolyDP(contour, epsilon, True)
```

If you run the preceding code using smoothen contours, the output will look like the following:

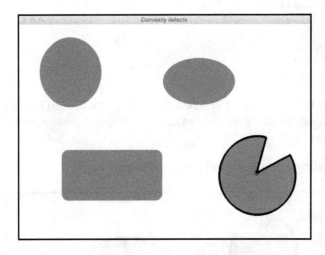

How to censor a shape?

Let's say you are dealing with images and you want to block out a particular shape. Now, you might say that you will use shape matching to identify the shape and then just block it out, right? But the problem here is that we don't have any template available. So, how do we go about doing this? Shape analysis comes in various forms, and we need to build our algorithm depending on the situation. Let's consider the following figure:

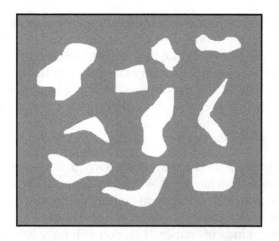

Let's say we want to identify all the boomerang shapes and then block them out without using any template images. As you can see, there are various other weird shapes in that image and the boomerang shapes are not really smooth. We need to identify the property that's going to differentiate the boomerang shape from the other shapes present. Let's consider the convex hull. If you take the ratio of the area of each shape to the area of the convex hull, we can see that this can be a distinguishing metric. This metric is called **solidity factor** in shape analysis. This metric will have a lower value for the boomerang shapes because of the empty area that will be left out, as shown in the following figure:

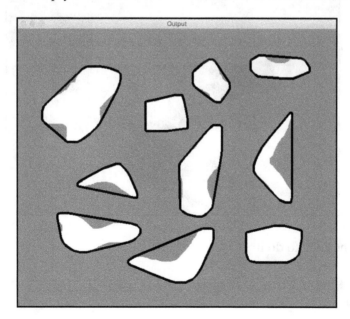

The black boundaries represent the convex hulls. Once we compute these values for all the shapes, how do we separate them out? Can we just use a fixed threshold to detect the boomerang shapes? Not really! We cannot have a fixed threshold value because you never know what kind of shape you might encounter later. So, a better approach would be to use **K-means clustering**. K-means is an unsupervised learning technique that can be used to separate out the input data into K classes. You can quickly brush up on K-means before proceeding further, at
`http://docs.opencv.org/master/de/d4d/tutorial_py_kmeans_understanding.html`.

We know that we want to separate the shapes into two groups, that is, boomerang shapes and other shapes. So, we know what our *K* will be in *K-means*. Once we use that and cluster the values, we pick the cluster with the lowest solidity factor and that will give us our boomerang shapes. Bear in mind that this approach works only in this particular case. If you are dealing with other kinds of shapes, then you will have to use some other metrics to make sure that the shape detection works. As we discussed earlier, it depends heavily on the situation. If you detect the shapes and block them out, it will look like this:

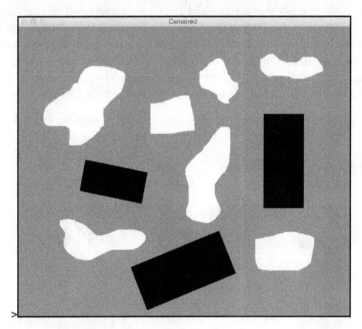

The following is the code to do it:

```
import sys
import cv2
import numpy as np
```

```
if __name__=='__main__':
    # Input image containing all the shapes
    img = cv2.imread(sys.argv[1])

    img_orig = np.copy(img)
    input_contours = get_all_contours(img)
    solidity_values = []

    # Compute solidity factors of all the contours
    for contour in input_contours:
        area_contour = cv2.contourArea(contour)
        convex_hull = cv2.convexHull(contour)
        area_hull = cv2.contourArea(convex_hull)
        solidity = float(area_contour)/area_hull
        solidity_values.append(solidity)

    # Clustering using KMeans
    criteria = (cv2.TERM_CRITERIA_EPS + cv2.TERM_CRITERIA_MAX_ITER, 10,
1.0)
    flags = cv2.KMEANS_RANDOM_CENTERS
    solidity_values = \
np.array(solidity_values).reshape((len(solidity_values),1)).astype('float32
')
    compactness, labels, centers = cv2.kmeans(solidity_values, 2, None,
criteria, 10, flags)

    closest_class = np.argmin(centers)
    output_contours = []
    for i in solidity_values[labels==closest_class]:
        index = np.where(solidity_values==i)[0][0]
        output_contours.append(input_contours[index])

    cv2.drawContours(img, output_contours, -1, (0,0,0), 3)
    cv2.imshow('Output', img)

    # Censoring
    for contour in output_contours:
        rect = cv2.minAreaRect(contour)
        box = cv2.boxPoints(rect)
        box = np.int0(box)
        cv2.drawContours(img_orig, [box], 0, (0,0,0), -1)

    cv2.imshow('Censored', img_orig)
    cv2.waitKey()
```

What is image segmentation?

Image segmentation is the process of separating an image into its constituent parts. It is an important step in many computer vision applications in the real world. There are many different ways of segmenting an image. When we segment an image, we separate the regions based on various metrics, such as color, texture, location, and so on. All the pixels within each region have something in common, depending on the metric we are using. Let's take a look at some of the popular approaches here.

To start with, we will be looking at a technique called **GrabCut**. It is an image segmentation method based on a more generic approach called **graph-cuts**. In the graph-cuts method, we consider the entire image to be a graph, and then we segment the graph based on the strength of the edges in that graph. We construct the graph by considering each pixel to be a node, and edges are constructed between the nodes, where edge weight is a function of the pixel values of those two nodes. Whenever there is a boundary, the pixel values are higher. Hence, the edge weights will also be higher. This graph is then segmented by minimizing the Gibbs energy of the graph. This is analogous to finding the maximum entropy segmentation. You can refer to the original paper to learn more about it, at `http://cvg.ethz.ch/teaching/cvl/2012/grabcut-siggraph04.pdf`.

Let's consider the following image:

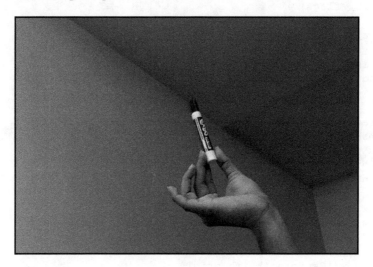

Let's select the region of interest:

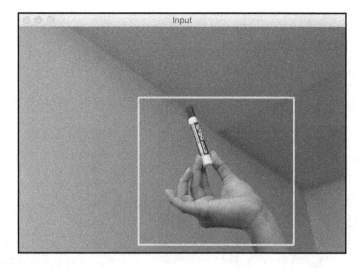

Once the image has been segmented, it will look something like this:

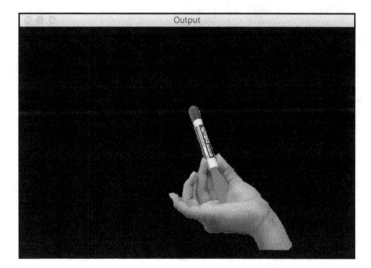

The following is the code to do this:

```python
import sys
import cv2
import numpy as np

# Draw rectangle based on the input selection
def draw_rectangle(event, x, y, flags, params):
    global x_init, y_init, drawing, top_left_pt, bottom_right_pt, img_orig

    # Detecting mouse button down event
    if event == cv2.EVENT_LBUTTONDOWN:
        drawing = True
        x_init, y_init = x, y

    # Detecting mouse movement
    elif event == cv2.EVENT_MOUSEMOVE:
        if drawing:
            top_left_pt, bottom_right_pt = (x_init,y_init), (x,y)
            img[y_init:y, x_init:x] = 255 - img_orig[y_init:y, x_init:x]
            cv2.rectangle(img, top_left_pt, bottom_right_pt, (0,255,0), 2)

    # Detecting mouse button up event
    elif event == cv2.EVENT_LBUTTONUP:
        drawing = False
        top_left_pt, bottom_right_pt = (x_init,y_init), (x,y)
        img[y_init:y, x_init:x] = 255 - img[y_init:y, x_init:x]
        cv2.rectangle(img, top_left_pt, bottom_right_pt, (0,255,0), 2)
        rect_final = (x_init, y_init, x-x_init, y-y_init)

        # Run Grabcut on the region of interest
        run_grabcut(img_orig, rect_final)

# Grabcut algorithm
def run_grabcut(img_orig, rect_final):
    # Initialize the mask
    mask = np.zeros(img_orig.shape[:2],np.uint8)

    # Extract the rectangle and set the region of
    # interest in the above mask
    x,y,w,h = rect_final
    mask[y:y+h, x:x+w] = 1

    # Initialize background and foreground models
    bgdModel = np.zeros((1,65), np.float64)
    fgdModel = np.zeros((1,65), np.float64)

    # Run Grabcut algorithm
```

```
    cv2.grabCut(img_orig, mask, rect_final, bgdModel, fgdModel, 5,
cv2.GC_INIT_WITH_RECT)

    # Extract new mask
    mask2 = np.where((mask==2)|(mask==0),0,1).astype('uint8')

    # Apply the above mask to the image
    img_orig = img_orig*mask2[:,:,np.newaxis]

    # Display the image
    cv2.imshow('Output', img_orig)

if __name__=='__main__':
    drawing = False
    top_left_pt, bottom_right_pt = (-1,-1), (-1,-1)

    # Read the input image
    img_orig = cv2.imread(sys.argv[1])
    img = img_orig.copy()

    cv2.namedWindow('Input')
    cv2.setMouseCallback('Input', draw_rectangle)

    while True:
        cv2.imshow('Input', img)
        c = cv2.waitKey(1)
        if c == 27:
            break

    cv2.destroyAllWindows()
```

How does it work?

We start with the seed points specified by the user. This is the bounding box within which we have the object of interest. Underneath the surface, the algorithm estimates the color distribution of the object and the background. The algorithm represents the color distribution of the image as a **Gaussian Mixture Markov Random Field** (**GMMRF**). You can refer to the detailed paper to learn more about GMMRF, at http://research.microsoft.com/pubs/67898/eccv04-GMMRF.pdf. We need the color distribution of both the object and the background, because we will be using this knowledge to separate the object. This information is used to find the maximum entropy segmentation by applying the min-cut algorithm to the Markov Random Field. Once we have this, we use the graph-cuts optimization method to infer the labels.

Watershed algorithm

OpenCV comes with default implementations of **watershed** algorithms, at `https://docs.opencv.org/trunk/d3/db4/tutorial_py_watershed.html`, which theory says that any grayscale image can be viewed as a topographic surface where high intensity denotes peaks and hills, while low intensity denotes valleys. This algorithm is pretty famous and there are a lot of implementations available out there.

Consider the following image:

Let's select the regions depending on their topographic surface:

If you run the watershed algorithm on this, the output will look something like this:

Sample code can be found on the link given previously, along with many other applications of the watershed algorithm.

Summary

In this chapter, we learned about contour analysis and image segmentation. We learned how to match shapes based on a template. We learned about the various different properties of shapes and how we can use them to identify different kinds of shapes. We discussed image segmentation and how we can use graph-based methods to segment regions in an image. We briefly discussed watershed transformation as well.

In the next chapter, we are going to discuss how to track an object in a live video.

8
Object Tracking

In this chapter, we are going to learn about tracking an object in a live video. We will discuss the different characteristics that can be used to track an object. We will also learn about the different methods and techniques for object tracking.

By the end of this chapter, you will know:

- How to use frame differencing
- How to use color spaces to track colored objects
- How to build an interactive object tracker
- How to build a feature tracker
- How to build a video surveillance system

Frame differencing

This is, possibly, the simplest technique we can use to see what parts of the video are moving. When we consider a live video stream, the difference between successive frames gives us a lot of information. The concept is fairly straightforward! We just take the difference between successive frames and display the differences.

If we move rapidly from left to right, we will see something like this:

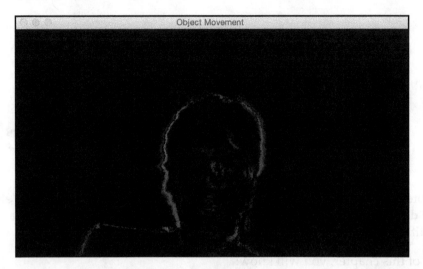

As you can see from the previous image, only the moving parts in the video get highlighted. This gives us a good starting point to see what areas are moving in the video. Here is the code to do this:

```python
import cv2

# Compute the frame difference
def frame_diff(prev_frame, cur_frame, next_frame):
    # Absolute difference between current frame and next frame
    diff_frames1 = cv2.absdiff(next_frame, cur_frame)

    # Absolute difference between current frame and
     # previous frame
    diff_frames2 = cv2.absdiff(cur_frame, prev_frame)

    # Return the result of bitwise 'AND' between the
    # above two resultant images to obtain a mask where
    # only the areas with white pixels are shown
    return cv2.bitwise_and(diff_frames1, diff_frames2)

# Capture the frame from webcam
def get_frame(cap, scaling_factor):
    # Capture the frame
    ret, frame = cap.read()

    # Resize the image
    frame = cv2.resize(frame, None, fx=scaling_factor,
```

```
                fy=scaling_factor, interpolation=cv2.INTER_AREA)

    return frame

if __name__=='__main__':
    cap = cv2.VideoCapture(0)
    scaling_factor = 0.5

    cur_frame, prev_frame, next_frame = None, None, None
    while True:
        frame = get_frame(cap, scaling_factor)
        prev_frame = cur_frame
        cur_frame = next_frame
        # Convert frame to grayscale image
        next_frame = cv2.cvtColor(frame, cv2.COLOR_RGB2GRAY)
        if prev_frame is not None:
            cv2.imshow("Object Movement", frame_diff(prev_frame, cur_frame,
next_frame))

        key = cv2.waitKey(delay=10)
        if key == 27:
            break

    cv2.destroyAllWindows()
```

A delay of 10 milliseconds has been used to have enough time between frames to generate an actual, significant difference.

Colorspace based tracking

Frame differencing gives us some useful information, but we cannot use it to build anything meaningful. In order to build a good object tracker, we need to understand what characteristics can be used to make our tracking robust and accurate. So, let's take a step in that direction and see how we can use **color spaces** to come up with a good tracker. As we have discussed in previous chapters, **HSV** color space is very informative when it comes to human perception. We can convert an image to the HSV space, and then use *color space thresholding* to track a given object.

Consider the following frame in the video:

If you run it through the color space filter and track the object, you will see something like this:

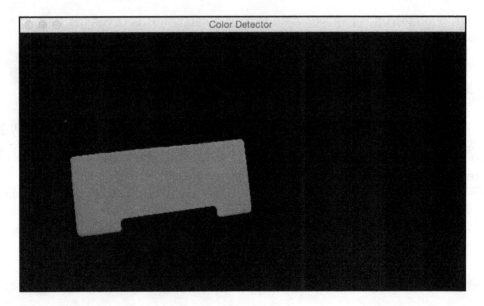

As we can see here, our tracker recognizes a particular object in the video, based on the color characteristics. In order to use this tracker, we need to know the color distribution of our target object. The following is the code:

```python
import cv2
import numpy as np

if __name__=='__main__':
    cap = cv2.VideoCapture(0)
    scaling_factor = 0.5

    # Define 'blue' range in HSV color space
    lower = np.array([60,100,100])
    upper = np.array([180,255,255])

    while True:
        frame = get_frame(cap, scaling_factor)

        # Convert the HSV color space
        hsv_frame = cv2.cvtColor(frame, cv2.COLOR_BGR2HSV)

        # Threshold the HSV image to get only blue color
        mask = cv2.inRange(hsv_frame, lower, upper)

        # Bitwise-AND mask and original image
        res = cv2.bitwise_and(frame, frame, mask=mask)
        res = cv2.medianBlur(res, ksize=5)

        cv2.imshow('Original image', frame)
        cv2.imshow('Color Detector', res)

        # Check if the user pressed ESC key
        c = cv2.waitKey(delay=10)
        if c == 27:
            break

    cv2.destroyAllWindows()
```

Building an interactive object tracker

The color space based tracker gives us the freedom to track a colored object, but we are also constrained to a predefined color. What if we just want to pick an object at random? How do we build an object tracker that can learn the characteristics of the selected object and just track it automatically? That is where the **CAMShift** algorithm, which stands for Continuously Adaptive Meanshift, comes into the picture. It's basically an improved version of the **Meanshift** algorithm.

The concept of Meanshift is actually nice and simple. Let's say we select a region of interest and we want our object tracker to track that object. In that region, we select a bunch of points based on the color histogram and compute the centroid. If the centroid lies at the center of this region, we know that the object hasn't moved. But if the centroid is not at the center of this region, then we know that the object is moving in some direction. The movement of the centroid controls the direction in which the object is moving. So, we move our bounding box to a new location so that the new centroid becomes the center of this bounding box. Hence, this algorithm is called Meanshift, because the mean (i.e. the centroid) is shifting. This way, we keep ourselves updated with the current location of the object.

But the problem with Meanshift is that the size of the bounding box is not allowed to change. When you move the object away from the camera, the object will appear smaller to the human eye, but Meanshift will not take this into account. The size of the bounding box will remain the same throughout the tracking session. Hence, we need to use CAMShift. The advantage of CAMShift is that it can adapt the size of the bounding box to the size of the object. Along with that, it can also keep track of the orientation of the object.

Let's consider the following frame, in which the object is highlighted in orange (the box in my hand):

Now that we have selected the object, the algorithm computes the *histogram backprojection* and extracts all the information. Let's move the object and see how it's getting tracked:

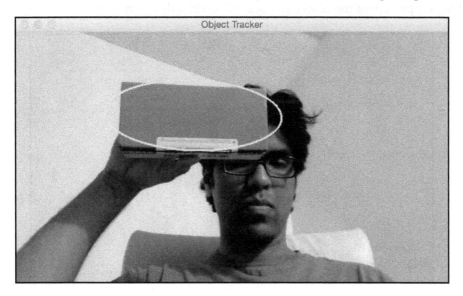

Looks like the object is getting tracked fairly well. Let's change the orientation and see if the tracking is maintained:

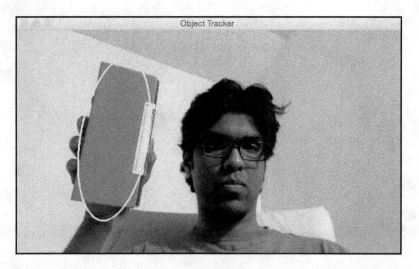

As we can see, the bounding ellipse has changed its location, as well as its orientation. Let's change the perspective of the object and see if it's still able to track it:

We are still good! The bounding ellipse has changed the aspect ratio to reflect the fact that the object looks skewed now (because of the perspective transformation).

The following is the code:

```
import sys
import cv2
import numpy as np

class ObjectTracker():
    def __init__(self):
        # Initialize the video capture object
        # 0 -> indicates that frame should be captured
        # from webcam
        self.cap = cv2.VideoCapture(0)

        # Capture the frame from the webcam
        ret, self.frame = self.cap.read()

        # Downsampling factor for the input frame
        self.scaling_factor = 0.8
        self.frame = cv2.resize(self.frame, None, fx=self.scaling_factor,
fy=self.scaling_factor, interpolation=cv2.INTER_AREA)

        cv2.namedWindow('Object Tracker')
        cv2.setMouseCallback('Object Tracker', self.mouse_event)

        self.selection = None
        self.drag_start = None
        self.tracking_state = 0

    # Method to track mouse events
    def mouse_event(self, event, x, y, flags, param):
        x, y = np.int16([x, y])

        # Detecting the mouse button down event
        if event == cv2.EVENT_LBUTTONDOWN:
            self.drag_start = (x, y)
            self.tracking_state = 0

        if self.drag_start:
            if event == cv2.EVENT_MOUSEMOVE:
                h, w = self.frame.shape[:2]
                xo, yo = self.drag_start
                x0, y0 = np.maximum(0, np.minimum([xo, yo], [x, y]))
                x1, y1 = np.minimum([w, h], np.maximum([xo, yo], [x, y]))
                self.selection = None

                if x1-x0 > 0 and y1-y0 > 0:
                    self.selection = (x0, y0, x1, y1)
```

```python
            elif event == cv2.EVENT_LBUTTONUP:
                self.drag_start = None
                if self.selection is not None:
                    self.tracking_state = 1

    # Method to start tracking the object
    def start_tracking(self):
        # Iterate until the user presses the Esc key
        while True:
            # Capture the frame from webcam
            ret, self.frame = self.cap.read()
            # Resize the input frame
            self.frame = cv2.resize(self.frame, None,
fx=self.scaling_factor, fy=self.scaling_factor,
interpolation=cv2.INTER_AREA)

            vis = self.frame.copy()

            # Convert to HSV color space
            hsv = cv2.cvtColor(self.frame, cv2.COLOR_BGR2HSV)

            # Create the mask based on predefined thresholds.
            mask = cv2.inRange(hsv, np.array((0., 60., 32.)),
np.array((180., 255., 255.)))

            if self.selection:
                x0, y0, x1, y1 = self.selection
                self.track_window = (x0, y0, x1-x0, y1-y0)
                hsv_roi = hsv[y0:y1, x0:x1]
                mask_roi = mask[y0:y1, x0:x1]

                # Compute the histogram
                hist = cv2.calcHist( [hsv_roi], [0], mask_roi, [16], [0,
180] )

                # Normalize and reshape the histogram
                cv2.normalize(hist, hist, 0, 255, cv2.NORM_MINMAX);
                self.hist = hist.reshape(-1)

                vis_roi = vis[y0:y1, x0:x1]
                cv2.bitwise_not(vis_roi, vis_roi)
                vis[mask == 0] = 0

            if self.tracking_state == 1:
                self.selection = None

                # Compute the histogram back projection
                prob = cv2.calcBackProject([hsv], [0], self.hist, [0, 180],
```

```
1)

            prob &= mask
            term_crit = ( cv2.TERM_CRITERIA_EPS |
cv2.TERM_CRITERIA_COUNT, 10, 1 )

            # Apply CAMShift on 'prob'
            track_box, self.track_window = cv2.CamShift(prob,
self.track_window, term_crit)

            # Draw an ellipse around the object
            cv2.ellipse(vis, track_box, (0, 255, 0), 2)

        cv2.imshow('Object Tracker', vis)

        c = cv2.waitKey(delay=5)
        if c == 27:
            break

    cv2.destroyAllWindows()

if __name__ == '__main__':
    ObjectTracker().start_tracking()
```

Feature-based tracking

Feature-based tracking refers to tracking individual feature points across successive frames in the video. We use a technique called **optical flow** to track these features. Optical flow is one of the most popular techniques in computer vision. We choose a bunch of feature points and track them through the video stream.

When we detect the feature points, we compute the displacement vectors and show the motion of those keypoints between consecutive frames. These vectors are called motion vectors. There are many ways to do this, but the Lucas-Kanade method is perhaps the most popular of all these techniques. You can learn more in the official OpenCV doc, at `https://docs.opencv.org/3.2.0/d7/d8b/tutorial_py_lucas_kanade.html`.

We start the process by extracting the feature points. For each feature point, we create 3x3 patches with the feature point in the center. The assumption here is that all the points within each patch will have a similar motion. We can adjust the size of this window depending on the problem at hand.

For each feature point in the current frame, we take the surrounding 3x3 patch as our reference point. For this patch, we look in its neighborhood in the previous frame to get the best match. This neighborhood is usually bigger than 3x3, because we want to get the patch that's closest to the patch under consideration. Now, the path from the center pixel of the matched patch in the previous frame to the center pixel of the patch under consideration in the current frame will become the motion vector. We do that for all the feature points and extract all the motion vectors.

Let's consider the following frame:

If I move in a horizontal direction, you will see the motion vectors in a horizontal direction:

If I move away from the webcam, you will see something like this:

First, we are going to implement a function to extract feature points from a given image to obtain moving vector using the previous frame:

```
def compute_feature_points(tracking_paths, prev_img, current_img):
    feature_points = [tp[-1] for tp in tracking_paths]
    # Vector of 2D points for which the flow needs to be found
    feature_points_0 = np.float32(feature_points).reshape(-1, 1, 2)

    feature_points_1, status_1, err_1 = cv2.calcOpticalFlowPyrLK(prev_img,
current_img, \
        feature_points_0, None, **tracking_params)
    feature_points_0_rev, status_2, err_2 =
cv2.calcOpticalFlowPyrLK(current_img, prev_img, \
        feature_points_1, None, **tracking_params)

    # Compute the difference of the feature points
    diff_feature_points = abs(feature_points_0-
feature_points_0_rev).reshape(-1, 2).max(-1)

    # threshold and keep only the good points
    good_points = diff_feature_points < 1
    return feature_points_1.reshape(-1, 2), good_points
```

Now we can implement a tracking method where, given a *region of interest* obtained and based on the feature points obtained from the method above, we can display motion vectors (tracking paths):

```python
# Extract area of interest based on the tracking_paths
# In case there is none, entire frame is used
def calculate_region_of_interest(frame, tracking_paths):
    mask = np.zeros_like(frame)
    mask[:] = 255
    for x, y in [np.int32(tp[-1]) for tp in tracking_paths]:
        cv2.circle(mask, (x, y), 6, 0, -1)
    return mask

def add_tracking_paths(frame, tracking_paths):
    mask = calculate_region_of_interest(frame, tracking_paths)

    # Extract good features to track. You can learn more
    # about the parameters here: http://goo.gl/BI2Kml
    feature_points = cv2.goodFeaturesToTrack(frame, mask = mask, maxCorners
= 500, \
        qualityLevel = 0.3, minDistance = 7, blockSize = 7)

    if feature_points is not None:
        for x, y in np.float32(feature_points).reshape(-1, 2):
            tracking_paths.append([(x, y)])

def start_tracking(cap, scaling_factor, num_frames_to_track,
num_frames_jump, tracking_params):
    tracking_paths = []
    frame_index = 0

    # Iterate until the user presses the ESC key
    while True:
        # read the input frame
        ret, frame = cap.read()

        # downsample the input frame
        frame = cv2.resize(frame, None, fx=scaling_factor,
fy=scaling_factor, \
interpolation=cv2.INTER_AREA)

        frame_gray = cv2.cvtColor(frame, cv2.COLOR_BGR2GRAY)
        output_img = frame.copy()

        if len(tracking_paths) > 0:
            prev_img, current_img = prev_gray, frame_gray
            # Compute feature points using optical flow. You can
```

```
            # refer to the documentation to learn more about the
            # parameters here: http://goo.gl/t6P4SE
            feature_points, good_points =
compute_feature_points(tracking_paths, \
                prev_img, current_img)

            new_tracking_paths = []
            for tp, (x, y), good_points_flag in \
                zip(tracking_paths, feature_points, good_points):
                if not good_points_flag: continue

                tp.append((x, y))

                # Using the queue structure i.e. first in, first out
                if len(tp) > num_frames_to_track: del tp[0]

                new_tracking_paths.append(tp)

                # draw green circles on top of the output image
                cv2.circle(output_img, (x, y), 3, (0, 255, 0), -1)

            tracking_paths = new_tracking_paths

            # draw green lines on top of the output image
            point_paths = [np.int32(tp) for tp in tracking_paths]
            cv2.polylines(output_img, point_paths, False, (0, 150, 0))

        # 'if' condition to skip every 'n'th frame
        if not frame_index % num_frames_jump:
            add_tracking_paths(frame_gray, tracking_paths)

        frame_index += 1
        prev_gray = frame_gray

        cv2.imshow('Optical Flow', output_img)

        # Check if the user pressed the ESC key
        c = cv2.waitKey(1)
        if c == 27:
            break
```

Here is the use of the code above to perform optical flow based tracking:

```
import cv2
import numpy as np


if __name__ == '__main__':
    # Capture the input frame
    cap = cv2.VideoCapture(1)

    # Downsampling factor for the image
    scaling_factor = 0.5

    # Number of frames to keep in the buffer when you
    # are tracking. If you increase this number,
    # feature points will have more "inertia"
    num_frames_to_track = 5

    # Skip every 'n' frames. This is just to increase the speed.
    num_frames_jump = 2

    # 'winSize' refers to the size of each patch. These patches
    # are the smallest blocks on which we operate and track
    # the feature points. You can read more about the parameters
    # here: http://goo.gl/ulwqLk
    tracking_params = dict(winSize = (11, 11), maxLevel = 2, \
        criteria = (cv2.TERM_CRITERIA_EPS | cv2.TERM_CRITERIA_COUNT, 10,
0.03))

    start_tracking(cap, scaling_factor, num_frames_to_track, \
        num_frames_jump, tracking_params)
    cv2.destroyAllWindows()
```

So, if you want to play around with it, you can let the user select a region of interest in the input video (like we did earlier). You can then extract feature points from this region of interest and track the object by drawing the bounding box. It will be a fun exercise!

Background subtraction

Background subtraction is very useful in video surveillance. Basically, the background subtraction technique performs really well for cases where we have to detect moving objects in a static scene. As the name indicates, this algorithm works by detecting the background and subtracting it from the current frame to obtain the foreground, that is, moving objects.

In order to detect moving objects, we need to build a model of the background first. This is not the same as frame differencing because we are actually modeling the background and using this model to detect moving objects. So, this performs much better than the simple frame differencing technique. This technique tries to detect static parts in the scene and then include them in the background model. So, it's an adaptive technique that can adjust according to the scene.

Let's consider the following image:

Now, as we gather more frames in this scene, every part of the image will gradually become a part of the background model. This is what we discussed earlier as well. If a scene is static, the model adapts itself to make sure the background model is updated. This is how it looks in the beginning:

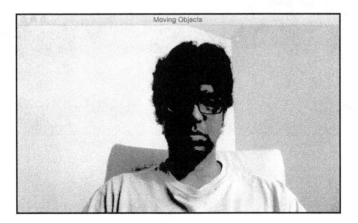

Notice how a part of my face has already become a part of the background model (the blackened region). The following screenshot shows what we'll see after a few seconds. If we keep going, everything eventually becomes part of the background model:

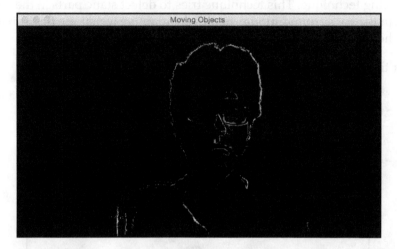

Now, if we introduce a new moving object, it will be detected clearly, as shown next:

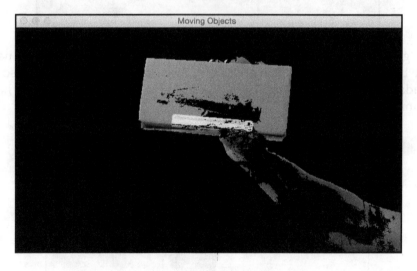

Here is the code to do this:

```python
import cv2
import numpy as np

# Capture the input frame
def get_frame(cap, scaling_factor=0.5):
    ret, frame = cap.read()

    # Resize the frame
    frame = cv2.resize(frame, None, fx=scaling_factor,
            fy=scaling_factor, interpolation=cv2.INTER_AREA)

    return frame

if __name__=='__main__':
    # Initialize the video capture object
    cap = cv2.VideoCapture(1)

    # Create the background subtractor object
    bgSubtractor = cv2.createBackgroundSubtractorMOG2()

    # This factor controls the learning rate of the algorithm.
    # The learning rate refers to the rate at which your model
    # will learn about the background. Higher value for
    # 'history' indicates a slower learning rate. You
    # can play with this parameter to see how it affects
    # the output.
    history = 100

    # Iterate until the user presses the ESC key
    while True:
        frame = get_frame(cap, 0.5)

        # Apply the background subtraction model to the input frame
        mask = bgSubtractor.apply(frame, learningRate=1.0/history)

        # Convert from grayscale to 3-channel RGB
        mask = cv2.cvtColor(mask, cv2.COLOR_GRAY2BGR)

        cv2.imshow('Input frame', frame)
        cv2.imshow('Moving Objects MOG', mask & frame)

        # Check if the user pressed the ESC key
        c = cv2.waitKey(delay=30)
        if c == 27:
            break
```

```
cap.release()
cv2.destroyAllWindows()
```

In the previous example, we used a background subtraction method known as **BackgroundSubtractorMOG**, which is a Gaussian Mixture-based Background/Foreground Segmentation Algorithm. In this algorithm, each of the background pixels is placed into a matrix and mixed by applying Gaussian distribution. Each of the colors will receive a weight to represent the time they stay in the scene; that way, colors that remain static are used to define the background:

```python
if __name__=='__main__':
    # Initialize the video capture object
    cap = cv2.VideoCapture(1)

    # Create the background subtractor object
    bgSubtractor= cv2.bgsegm.createBackgroundSubtractorGMG()
    kernel = cv2.getStructuringElement(cv2.MORPH_ELLIPSE, ksize=(3,3))

    # Iterate until the user presses the ESC key
    while True:
        frame = get_frame(cap, 0.5)

        # Apply the background subtraction model to the input frame
        mask = bgSubtractor.apply(frame)
        # Removing noise from background
        mask = cv2.morphologyEx(mask, cv2.MORPH_OPEN, kernel)

        cv2.imshow('Input frame', frame)
        cv2.imshow('Moving Objects', mask)

        # Check if the user pressed the ESC key
        c = cv2.waitKey(delay=30)
        if c == 27:
            break

    cap.release()
    cv2.destroyAllWindows()
```

There are other alternatives which might perform better; for instance, removing image noise, which is the case of the BackgroundSubtractorGMG. If you want to know more about them, go to https://docs.opencv.org/3.0-beta/doc/py_tutorials/py_video/py_bg_subtraction/py_bg_subtraction.html.

Summary

In this chapter, we learned about object tracking. We learned how to get motion information using frame differencing, and how it can be limiting when we want to track different types of objects. We learned about color space thresholding and how it can be used to track colored objects. We discussed clustering techniques for object tracking and how we can build an interactive object tracker using the CAMShift algorithm. We discussed how to track features in a video and how we can use optical flow to achieve the same. We learned about background subtraction and how it can be used for video surveillance.

In the next chapter, we are going to discuss object recognition, and how we can build a visual search engine.

9
Object Recognition

In this chapter, we are going to learn about object recognition and how we can use it to build a visual search engine. We will discuss feature detection, building feature vectors, and using machine learning to build a classifier. We will learn how to use these different blocks to build an object recognition system.

By the end of this chapter, you will know:

- The difference between object detection and object recognition
- What a dense feature detector is
- What a visual dictionary is
- How to build a feature vector
- What supervised and unsupervised learning are
- What support vector machines are and how to use them to build a classifier
- How to recognize an object in an unknown image

Object detection versus object recognition

Before we proceed, we need to understand what we are going to discuss in this chapter. You must have frequently heard the terms *object detection* and *object recognition*, and they are often mistaken to be the same thing. There is a very distinct difference between the two.

Object detection refers to detecting the presence of a particular object in a given scene. We don't know what the object might be. For instance, we discussed face detection in `Chapter 4`, *Detecting and Tracking Different Body Parts*. During the discussion, we only detected whether or not a face was present in the given image. We didn't recognize the person! The reason we didn't recognize the person is because we didn't care about that in our discussion. Our goal was to find the location of the face in the given image. Commercial face recognition systems employ both face detection and face recognition to identify a person. First, we need to locate the face, and then run the face recognizer on the cropped face.

Object recognition is the process of identifying an object in a given image. For instance, an object recognition system can tell you if a given image contains a dress or a pair of shoes. In fact, we can train an object recognition system to identify many different objects. The problem is that object recognition is a really difficult problem to solve. It has eluded computer vision researchers for decades now and has become the holy grail of computer vision. Humans can identify a wide variety of objects very easily. We do it every day and we do it effortlessly, but computers are unable to do it with that kind of accuracy.

Let's consider the following image of a latte cup:

An object detector will give you the following information:

Now, consider the following image of a teacup:

If you run it through an object detector, you will see the following result:

As you can see, the object detector detects the presence of the teacup, but nothing more than that. If you train an object recognizer, it will give you the following information, as shown in the following image:

If you consider the second image, it will give you the following information:

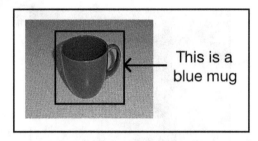

As you can see, a perfect object recognizer would give you all the information associated with that object. An object recognizer functions more accurately if it knows where the object is located. If you have a big image and the cup is a small part of it, then the object recognizer might not be able to recognize it. Hence, the first step is to detect the object and get the bounding box. Once we have that, we can run an object recognizer to extract more information.

What is a dense feature detector?

In order to extract a meaningful amount of information from the images, we need to make sure our feature extractor extracts features from all parts of a given image. Consider the following image:

If you extract features using a feature extractor as we did in `Chapter 5`, *Extracting Features from an Image*, it will look like this:

If you used to use the `cv2.FeaturetureDetector_create("Dense")` detector, unfortunately, that was removed from OpenCV 3.2 onwards, so we would need to implement our own one iterating over the grid and obtaining the keypoints:

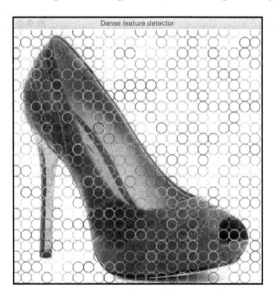

We can control the density as well. Let's make it sparse:

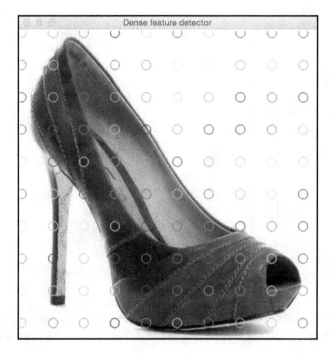

By doing this, we can make sure that every single part in the image is processed. Here is the code to do it:

```
import sys
import cv2
import numpy as np

class DenseDetector():
    def __init__(self, step_size=20, feature_scale=20, img_bound=20):
        # Create a dense feature detector
        self.initXyStep = step_size
        self.initFeatureScale = feature_scale
        self.initImgBound = img_bound

    def detect(self, img):
        keypoints = []
        rows, cols = img.shape[:2]
        for x in range(self.initImgBound, rows, self.initFeatureScale):
            for y in range(self.initImgBound, cols, self.initFeatureScale):
                keypoints.append(cv2.KeyPoint(float(x), float(y),
self.initXyStep))
```

```
            return keypoints

class SIFTDetector():
    def __init__(self):
        self.detector = cv2.xfeatures2d.SIFT_create()

    def detect(self, img):
        # Convert to grayscale
        gray_image = cv2.cvtColor(img, cv2.COLOR_BGR2GRAY)
        # Detect keypoints using SIFT
        return self.detector.detect(gray_image, None)

if __name__=='__main__':
    input_image = cv2.imread(sys.argv[1])
    input_image_dense = np.copy(input_image)
    input_image_sift = np.copy(input_image)

    keypoints = DenseDetector(20,20,5).detect(input_image)
    # Draw keypoints on top of the input image
    input_image_dense = cv2.drawKeypoints(input_image_dense, keypoints,
None,\
        flags=cv2.DRAW_MATCHES_FLAGS_DRAW_RICH_KEYPOINTS)
    # Display the output image
    cv2.imshow('Dense feature detector', input_image_dense)

    keypoints = SIFTDetector().detect(input_image)
    # Draw SIFT keypoints on the input image
    input_image_sift = cv2.drawKeypoints(input_image_sift, keypoints,
None,\
        flags=cv2.DRAW_MATCHES_FLAGS_DRAW_RICH_KEYPOINTS)
    # Display the output image
    cv2.imshow('SIFT detector', input_image_sift)

    # Wait until user presses a key
    cv2.waitKey()
```

This gives us close control over the amount of information that gets extracted. When we use a SIFT detector, some parts of the image are neglected. This works well when we are dealing with the detection of prominent features, but when we are building an object recognizer, we need to evaluate all parts of the image. Hence, we use a dense detector and then extract features from those keypoints.

What is a visual dictionary?

We will be using the *Bag of Words* model to build our object recognizer. Each image is represented as a histogram of visual words. These visual words are basically the N centroids built using all the keypoints extracted from training images. The pipeline is as shown in the image that follows:

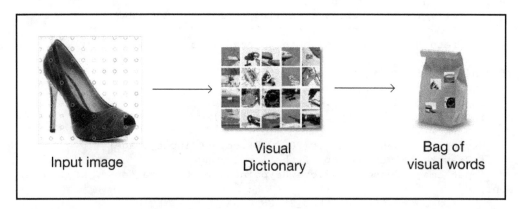

Input image   Visual Dictionary   Bag of visual words

From each training image, we detect a set of keypoints and extract features for each of those keypoints. Every image will give rise to a different number of keypoints. In order to train a classifier, each image must be represented using a fixed length feature vector. This feature vector is merely a histogram, where each bin corresponds to a visual word.

When we extract all the features from all the keypoints in the training images, we perform K-means clustering and extract N centroids. This N is the length of the feature vector of a given image. Each image will now be represented as a histogram, where each bin corresponds to one of the N centroids. For simplicity, let's say that N is set to four. Now, in a given image, we extract K keypoints. Out of these K keypoints, some of them will be closest to the first centroid, some of them will be closest to the second centroid, and so on. So, we build a histogram based on the closest centroid to each keypoint. This histogram becomes our feature vector. This process is called **vector quantization**.

To understand vector quantization, let's consider an example. Assume we have an image and we've extracted a certain number of feature points from it. Now our goal is to represent this image in the form of a feature vector. Consider the following image:

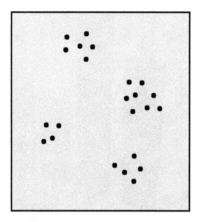

As you can see, we have four centroids. Bear in mind that the points shown in the figures represent the feature space and not the actual geometric locations of those feature points in the image. It is shown this way in the preceding figure so that it's easy to visualize. Points from many different geometric locations in an image can be close to each other in the feature space. Our goal is to represent this image as a histogram, where each bin corresponds to one of these centroids. This way, no matter how many feature points we extract from an image, it will always be converted to a fixed length feature vector. So, we *round off* each feature point to its nearest centroid, as shown in the following image:

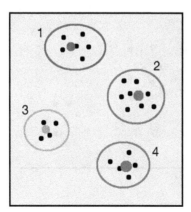

If you build a histogram for this image, it will look like this:

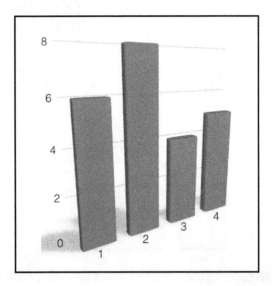

Now, if you consider a different image with a different distribution of feature points, it will look like this:

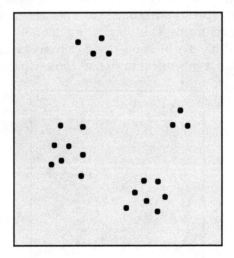

The clusters would look like the following:

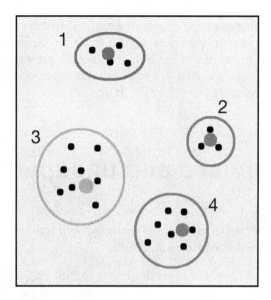

The histogram would look like this:

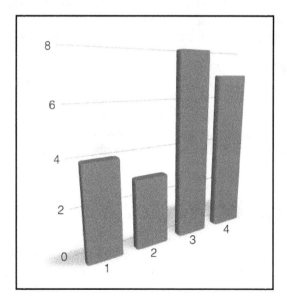

As you can see, the histograms are very different for the two images even though the points seem to be randomly distributed. This is a very powerful technique and it's widely used in computer vision and signal processing. There are many different ways to do this and the accuracy depends on how fine-grained you want it to be. If you increase the number of centroids, you will be able to represent the image better, thereby increasing the uniqueness of your feature vector. Having said that, it's important to mention that you cannot just keep increasing the number of centroids indefinitely. If you do that, it will become too noisy and lose its power.

What is supervised and unsupervised learning?

If you are familiar with the basics of machine learning, you will certainly know what supervised and unsupervised learning is all about.

To give a quick refresher, **supervised learning** refers to building a function based on labeled samples. For example, if we are building a system to separate dress images from footwear images, we first need to build a database and label it. We need to tell our algorithm what images correspond to dresses and what images correspond to footwear. Based on this data, the algorithm will learn how to identify dresses and footwear so that when an unknown image comes in, it can recognize what's inside that image.

Unsupervised learning is the opposite of what we just discussed. There is no labeled data available here. Let's say we have a bunch of images, and we just want to separate them into three groups. We don't know what the criteria will be. So, an unsupervised learning algorithm will try to separate the given set of data into three groups in the best possible way. The reason we are discussing this is because we will be using a combination of supervised and unsupervised learning to build our object recognition system.

What are support vector machines?

Support vector machines (SVM) are supervised learning models that are very popular in the realm of machine learning. SVMs are really good at analyzing labeled data and detecting patterns. Given a bunch of data points and the associated labels, SVMs will build the separating hyperplanes in the best possible way.

Wait a minute, what are hyperplanes? To understand that, let's consider the following figure:

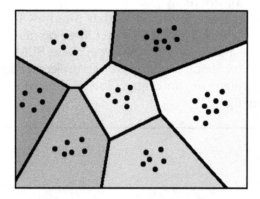

As you can see, the points are being separated by line boundaries that are equidistant from the points. This is easy to visualize in two dimensions. If it were in three dimensions, the separators would be planes. When we build features for images, the length of the feature vectors is usually in the six-digit range. So, when we go to such a high dimensional space, the equivalent of lines would be hyperplanes. Once the hyperplanes are formulated, we use this mathematical model to classify unknown data, based on where it falls on this map.

What if we cannot separate the data with simple straight lines?

There is something called the **kernel trick** that we use in SVMs. Consider the following image:

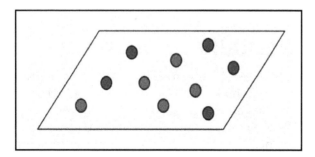

As we can see, we cannot draw a simple straight line to separate the red points from the blue points. Coming up with a nice curvy boundary that will satisfy all the points is prohibitively expensive. SVMs are really good at drawing straight lines. So, what's our answer here? The good thing about SVMs is that they can draw these straight lines in any number of dimensions. So technically, if you project these points into a high dimensional space, where they can be separated by a simple hyperplane, SVMs will come up with an exact boundary. Once we have that boundary, we can project it back to the original space. The projection of this hyperplane on our original lower dimensional space looks curvy, as we can see in the following figure:

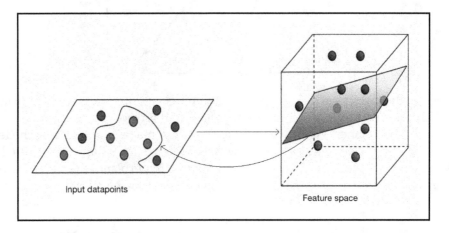

Input datapoints

Feature space

The topic of SVMs is really deep and we will not be able to discuss it in detail here. If you are really interested, there is a ton of material available online. You can go through a simple tutorial to understand it better. Also OpenCV official documentation contains several examples for better understanding: `https://docs.opencv.org/3.0-beta/modules/ml/doc/support_vector_machines.html`.

How do we actually implement this?

We have now arrived at the core. The previous introduction was necessary because it gives you the background required to build an object detection and recognition system. Now, let's build an object recognizer that can recognize whether the given image contains a dress, a pair of shoes, or a bag. We can easily extend this system to detect any number of items. We are starting with three distinct items so that you can start experimenting with it later.

Before we start, we need to make sure that we have a set of training images. There are many databases available online, where the images are already arranged into groups. **Caltech256** is perhaps one of the most popular databases for object recognition. You can download it from `http://www.vision.caltech.edu/Image_Datasets/Caltech256`. Create a folder called `images` and create three sub folders inside it—that is, `dress`, `footwear`, and `bag`. Inside each of those sub folders, add 20 images corresponding to that item. You can just download these images from the internet, but make sure those images have a clean background.

For example, a dress image would like this:

A footwear image would look like this:

A bag image would look like this:

Now that we have 60 training images, we are ready to start. As a side note, object recognition systems actually need tens of thousands of training images in order to perform well in the real world. Since we are building an object recognizer to detect three types of objects, we will take only 20 training images per object. Adding more training images will increase the accuracy and robustness of our system.

The first step here is to extract feature vectors from all the training images and build the visual dictionary (also known as codebook).

First, reusing our previous `DenseDetector` class, plus SIFT feature detector:

```
class SIFTExtractor():
    def __init__(self):
        self.extractor = cv2.xfeatures2d.SIFT_create()

    def compute(self, image, kps):
        if image is None:
            print "Not a valid image"
            raise TypeError

        gray_image = cv2.cvtColor(image, cv2.COLOR_BGR2GRAY)
        kps, des = self.extractor.detectAndCompute(gray_image, None)
        return kps, des
```

Then our `Quantizer` class calculates vector quantization and builds the feature vector:

```
from sklearn.cluster import KMeans

# Vector quantization
class Quantizer(object):
    def __init__(self, num_clusters=32):
        self.num_dims = 128
        self.extractor = SIFTExtractor()
        self.num_clusters = num_clusters
        self.num_retries = 10

    def quantize(self, datapoints):
        # Create KMeans object
        kmeans = KMeans(self.num_clusters,
                        n_init=max(self.num_retries, 1),
                        max_iter=10, tol=1.0)

        # Run KMeans on the datapoints
        res = kmeans.fit(datapoints)

        # Extract the centroids of those clusters
        centroids = res.cluster_centers_

        return kmeans, centroids

    def normalize(self, input_data):
        sum_input = np.sum(input_data)
        if sum_input > 0:
```

```
              return input_data / sum_input
          else:
              return input_data

      # Extract feature vector from the image
      def get_feature_vector(self, img, kmeans, centroids):
          kps = DenseDetector().detect(img)
          kps, fvs = self.extractor.compute(img, kps)
          labels = kmeans.predict(fvs)
          fv = np.zeros(self.num_clusters)

          for i, item in enumerate(fvs):
              fv[labels[i]] += 1

          fv_image = np.reshape(fv, ((1, fv.shape[0])))
          return self.normalize(fv_image)
```

Reusing previous implementations, another required class will be the `FeatureExtractor` class, which is designed to extract the centroids of each of the images:

```
class FeatureExtractor(object):
    def extract_image_features(self, img):
        # Dense feature detector
        kps = DenseDetector().detect(img)

        # SIFT feature extractor
        kps, fvs = SIFTExtractor().compute(img, kps)

        return fvs

    # Extract the centroids from the feature points
    def get_centroids(self, input_map, num_samples_to_fit=10):
        kps_all = []

        count = 0
        cur_label = ''
        for item in input_map:
            if count >= num_samples_to_fit:
                if cur_label != item['label']:
                    count = 0
                else:
                    continue

            count += 1

            if count == num_samples_to_fit:
                print("Built centroids for", item['label'])
```

```
        cur_label = item['label']
        img = cv2.imread(item['image'])
        img = resize_to_size(img, 150)

        num_dims = 128
        fvs = self.extract_image_features(img)
        kps_all.extend(fvs)

    kmeans, centroids = Quantizer().quantize(kps_all)
    return kmeans, centroids

def get_feature_vector(self, img, kmeans, centroids):
    return Quantizer().get_feature_vector(img, kmeans, centroids)
```

The following script will provide us a dictionary of features to classify future images:

```
#########################
# create_features.py
#########################

import os
import sys
import argparse
import json

import cv2
import numpy as np

import cPickle as pickle
# In case of Python 2.7 use:
# import cPickle as pickle

def build_arg_parser():
    parser = argparse.ArgumentParser(description='Creates features for
given images')
    parser.add_argument("--samples", dest="cls", nargs="+",
action="append", required=True,\
        help="Folders containing the training images.\nThe first element
needs to be the class label.")
    parser.add_argument("--codebook-file", dest='codebook_file',
required=True,
        help="Base file name to store the codebook")
    parser.add_argument("--feature-map-file", dest='feature_map_file',
required=True,\
        help="Base file name to store the feature map")

    return parser
```

```python
# Loading the images from the input folder
def load_input_map(label, input_folder):
    combined_data = []

    if not os.path.isdir(input_folder):
        raise IOError("The folder " + input_folder + " doesn't exist")

    # Parse the input folder and assign the labels
    for root, dirs, files in os.walk(input_folder):
        for filename in (x for x in files if x.endswith('.jpg')):
            combined_data.append({'label': label, 'image':
                os.path.join(root, filename)})

    return combined_data

def extract_feature_map(input_map, kmeans, centroids):
    feature_map = []

    for item in input_map:
        temp_dict = {}
        temp_dict['label'] = item['label']

        print("Extracting features for", item['image'])
        img = cv2.imread(item['image'])
        img = resize_to_size(img, 150)

        temp_dict['feature_vector'] =
FeatureExtractor().get_feature_vector(img, kmeans, centroids)

        if temp_dict['feature_vector'] is not None:
            feature_map.append(temp_dict)

    return feature_map

# Resize the shorter dimension to 'new_size'
# while maintaining the aspect ratio
def resize_to_size(input_image, new_size=150):
    h, w = input_image.shape[0], input_image.shape[1]
    ds_factor = new_size / float(h)

    if w < h:
        ds_factor = new_size / float(w)

    new_size = (int(w * ds_factor), int(h * ds_factor))
    return cv2.resize(input_image, new_size)

if __name__=='__main__':
    args = build_arg_parser().parse_args()
```

```
input_map = []
for cls in args.cls:
    assert len(cls) >= 2, "Format for classes is `<label> file`"
    label = cls[0]
    input_map += load_input_map(label, cls[1])

# Building the codebook
print("===== Building codebook =====")
kmeans, centroids = FeatureExtractor().get_centroids(input_map)
if args.codebook_file:
    with open(args.codebook_file, 'wb') as f:
        print('kmeans', kmeans)
        print('centroids', centroids)
        pickle.dump((kmeans, centroids), f)

# Input data and labels
print("===== Building feature map =====")
feature_map = extract_feature_map(input_map, kmeans,
 centroids)
if args.feature_map_file:
    with open(args.feature_map_file, 'wb') as f:
        pickle.dump(feature_map, f)
```

What happened inside the code?

The first thing we need to do is extract the centroids. This is how we are going to build our visual dictionary. The `get_centroids` method in the `FeatureExtractor` class is designed to do this. We keep collecting the image features extracted from keypoints until we have a sufficient number of them. Since we are using a dense detector, 10 images should be sufficient. The reason we are just taking 10 images is because they will give rise to a large number of features. The centroids will not change much even if you add more feature points.

Once we've extracted the centroids, we are ready to move on to the next step of feature extraction. The set of centroids is our visual dictionary. The function, `extract_feature_map`, will extract a feature vector from each image and associate it with the corresponding label. The reason we do this is because we need this mapping to train our classifier. We need a set of keypoints, and each keypoint should be associated with a label. So, we start from an image, extract the feature vector, and then associate it with the corresponding label (such as bag, dress, or footwear).

The `Quantizer` class is designed to achieve vector quantization and build the feature vector. For each keypoint extracted from the image, the `get_feature_vector` method finds the closest visual word in our dictionary. By doing this, we end up building a histogram based on our visual dictionary. Each image is now represented as a combination from a set of visual words. Hence the name, **Bag of Words**.

The next step is to train the classifier using these features. For that we implement another class:

```python
from sklearn.multiclass import OneVsOneClassifier
from sklearn.svm import LinearSVC
from sklearn import preprocessing

# To train the classifier
class ClassifierTrainer(object):
    def __init__(self, X, label_words):
        # Encoding the labels (words to numbers)
        self.le = preprocessing.LabelEncoder()

        # Initialize One versus One Classifier using a linear kernel
        self.clf = OneVsOneClassifier(LinearSVC(random_state=0))

        y = self._encodeLabels(label_words)
        X = np.asarray(X)
        self.clf.fit(X, y)

    # Predict the output class for the input datapoint
    def _fit(self, X):
        X = np.asarray(X)
        return self.clf.predict(X)

    # Encode the labels (convert words to numbers)
    def _encodeLabels(self, labels_words):
        self.le.fit(labels_words)
        return np.array(self.le.transform(labels_words),
          dtype=np.float32)

    # Classify the input datapoint
    def classify(self, X):
        labels_nums = self._fit(X)
        labels_words = self.le.inverse_transform([int(x) for x in
          labels_nums])
        return labels_words
```

Now, based on our previous feature dictionary we generate the SVM file:

```
###############
# training.py
###############

import os
import sys
import argparse

import _pickle as pickle
import numpy as np

def build_arg_parser():
    parser = argparse.ArgumentParser(description='Trains the classifier
models')
    parser.add_argument("--feature-map-file", dest="feature_map_file",
required=True,\
        help="Input pickle file containing the feature map")
    parser.add_argument("--svm-file", dest="svm_file", required=False,\
        help="Output file where the pickled SVM model will be stored")
    return parser
if __name__=='__main__':
    args = build_arg_parser().parse_args()
    feature_map_file = args.feature_map_file
    svm_file = args.svm_file

    # Load the feature map
    with open(feature_map_file, 'rb') as f:
        feature_map = pickle.load(f)

    # Extract feature vectors and the labels
    labels_words = [x['label'] for x in feature_map]

    # Here, 0 refers to the first element in the
    # feature_map, and 1 refers to the second
    # element in the shape vector of that element
    # (which gives us the size)
    dim_size = feature_map[0]['feature_vector'].shape[1]

    X = [np.reshape(x['feature_vector'], (dim_size,)) for x in feature_map]

    # Train the SVM
    svm = ClassifierTrainer(X, labels_words)
    if args.svm_file:
        with open(args.svm_file, 'wb') as f:
            pickle.dump(svm, f)
```

Notice we are writing/reading in binary mode, that is the reason for the use of rb and wb mode when a file is being opened.

How did we build the trainer?

We use the `scikit-learn` package to build the SVM model and `scipy` for mathematical optimization tools. You can install it as follows:

```
$ pip install scikit-learn scipy
```

We start with labeled data and feed it to the `OneVsOneClassifier` method. We have a `classify` method that classifies an input image and associates a label with it.

Let's give this a trial run, shall we? Make sure you have a folder called `images`, where you have the training images for the three classes. Create a folder called `models`, where the learning models will be stored. Run the following commands on your terminal to create the features and train the classifier:

```
$ python create_features.py --samples bag images/bag/ --samples dress
images/dress/ --samples footwear images/footwear/ --codebook-file
models/codebook.pkl --feature-map-file models/feature_map.pkl

$ python training.py --feature-map-file models/feature_map.pkl
--svm-file models/svm.pkl
```

Now that the classifier has been trained, we just need a module to classify the input image and detect the object inside:

```python
import create_features as cf
from training import ClassifierTrainer

# Classifying an image
class ImageClassifier(object):
    def __init__(self, svm_file, codebook_file):
        # Load the SVM classifier
        with open(svm_file, 'rb') as f:
            self.svm = pickle.load(f)

        # Load the codebook
        with open(codebook_file, 'rb') as f:
            self.kmeans, self.centroids = pickle.load(f)

    # Method to get the output image tag
    def getImageTag(self, img):
        # Resize the input image
```

```
        img = cf.resize_to_size(img)

        # Extract the feature vector
        feature_vector = cf.FeatureExtractor().get_feature_vector(img,
self.kmeans, \
            self.centroids)

        # Classify the feature vector and get the output tag
        image_tag = self.svm.classify(feature_vector)

        return image_tag
```

Here is the script to classify data, which can tag an image based on our previous training process:

```
##############
# classify_data.py
##############
import os
import sys
import argparse
import _pickle as pickle

import cv2
import numpy as np

def build_arg_parser():
    parser = argparse.ArgumentParser(description='Extracts features from
each line and classifies the data')
    parser.add_argument("--input-image", dest="input_image",
required=True,\
        help="Input image to be classified")
    parser.add_argument("--svm-file", dest="svm_file", required=True,\
        help="File containing the trained SVM model")
    parser.add_argument("--codebook-file", dest="codebook_file",
required=True,\
        help="File containing the codebook")
    return parser

if __name__=='__main__':
    args = build_arg_parser().parse_args()
    svm_file = args.svm_file
    codebook_file = args.codebook_file
    input_image = cv2.imread(args.input_image)

    tag = ImageClassifier(svm_file, codebook_file).getImageTag(input_image)
    print("Output class:", tag)
```

We are all set! We just extract the `feature` vector from the input image and use it as the input argument to the classifier. Let's go ahead and see if this works. Download a random footwear image from the internet and make sure it has a clean background. Run the following command by replacing `new_image.jpg` with the right filename:

```
$ python classify_data.py --input-image new_image.jpg --svm-file
models/svm.pkl --codebook-file models/codebook.pkl
```

We can use the same technique to build a visual search engine. A visual search engine looks at the input image and shows a bunch of images that are similar to it. We can reuse the object recognition framework to build this. Extract the feature vector from the input image, and compare it with all the feature vectors in the training dataset. Pick out the top matches and display the results. This is a simple way of doing things!

In the real world, we have to deal with billions of images. So, you cannot afford to search through every single image before you display the output. There are a lot of algorithms that are used to make sure that this is efficient and fast in the real world. Deep learning is being used extensively in this field and it has shown a lot of promise in recent years. It is a branch of machine learning that focuses on learning optimal representation of data, so that it becomes easier for the machines to *learn* new tasks. You can learn more about it at: `http://deeplearning.net`.

Summary

In this chapter, we learned how to build an object recognition system. The differences between object detection and object recognition were discussed in detail. We learned about the dense feature detector, visual dictionary, vector quantization, and how to use these concepts to build a feature vector. The concepts of supervised and unsupervised learning were discussed. We talked about Support Vector Machines and how we can use them to build a classifier. We learned how to recognize an object in an unknown image, and how we can extend that concept to build a visual search engine.

In the next chapter, we are going to discuss stereo imaging and 3D reconstruction. We will talk about how we can build a depth map and extract the 3D information from a given scene.

10
Augmented Reality

In this chapter, you are going to learn about augmented reality and how you can use it to build cool applications. We will discuss pose estimation and plane tracking. You will learn how to map the coordinates from 3D to 2D, and how we can overlay graphics on top of a live video.

By the end of this chapter, you will know:

- The premise of augmented reality
- What pose estimation is
- How to track a planar object
- How to map coordinates from 3D to 2D
- How to overlay graphics on top of a video in real time

What is the premise of augmented reality?

Before we jump into all the fun stuff, let's understand what augmented reality means. You will have probably seen the term augmented reality being used in a variety of contexts. So, we should understand the premise of augmented reality before we start discussing the implementation details. Augmented reality refers to the superimposition of computer-generated input, such as imagery, sounds, graphics, and text, on top of the real world.

Augmented reality tries to blur the line between what's real and what's computer-generated by seamlessly merging information and enhancing what we see and feel. It is actually closely related to a concept called mediated reality, where a computer modifies our view of reality. As a result of this, the technology works by enhancing our current perception of reality. Now, the challenge here is to make it look seamless to the user. It's easy to just overlay something on top of the input video, but we need to make it look as though it is part of the video. The user should feel that the computer-generated input closely reflects the real world. This is what we want to achieve when we build an augmented reality system.

Computer vision research in this context explores how we can apply computer-generated imagery to live video streams so that we can enhance the perception of the real world. Augmented reality technology has a wide variety of applications, including, but not limited to, head-mounted displays, automobiles, data visualization, gaming, construction, and so on. Now that we have powerful smartphones and smarter machines, we can build high-end augmented reality applications with ease.

What does an augmented reality system look like?

Let's consider the following figure:

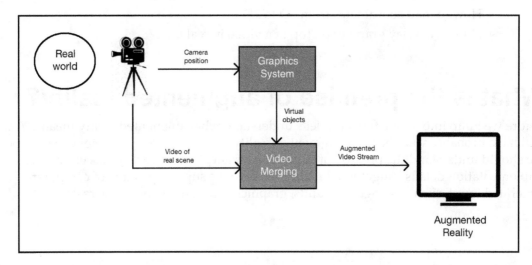

As we can see here, the camera captures real-world video to get the reference point. The graphics system generates the virtual objects that need to be overlaid on top of the video. Now, the video-merging block is where all the magic happens. This block should be smart enough to understand how to overlay the virtual objects on top of the real world in the best way possible.

Geometric transformations for augmented reality

The result of augmented reality is amazing, but there are a lot of mathematical things going on underneath. Augmented reality utilizes a lot of geometric transformations and associated mathematical functions to make sure everything looks smooth. When talking about a live video for augmented reality, we need to precisely register the virtual objects on top of the real world. To understand this better, let's think of it as an alignment of two cameras: the real one through which we see the world, and the virtual one that projects the computer-generated graphical objects.

In order to build an augmented reality system, the following geometric transformations need to be established:

- **Object-to-scene**: This transformation refers to transforming the 3D coordinates of a virtual object and expressing them in the coordinate frame of our real-world scene. This ensures that we are placing the virtual object in the right location.
- **Scene-to-camera**: This transformation refers to the pose of the camera in the real world. By *pose*, we mean the orientation and location of the camera. We need to estimate the point of view of the camera so that we know how to overlay the virtual object.
- **Camera-to-image**: This refers to the calibration parameters of the camera. This defines how we can project a 3D object onto a 2D image plane. This is the image that we will actually see in the end.

Consider the following image:

As we can see here, the car is trying to fit into the scene but it looks very artificial. If we don't convert the coordinates in the right way, the car will look unnatural. This is what we were saying about object-to-scene transformation! Once we transform the 3D coordinates of the virtual object into the coordinate frame of the real world, we need to estimate the pose of the camera:

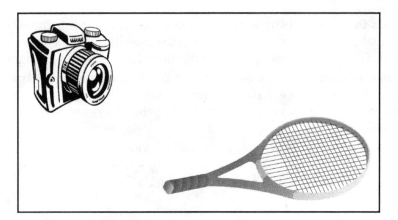

We need to understand the position and rotation of the camera because that's what the user will see. Once we estimate the camera pose, we are ready to put this 3D scene on a 2D image:

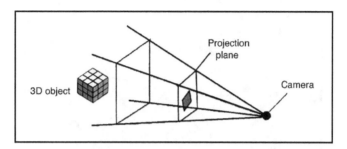

Once we have these transformations, we can build the complete system.

What is pose estimation?

Before we proceed, we need to understand how to estimate the camera pose. This is a very critical step in an augmented reality system and we need to get it right if we want our experience to be seamless. In the world of augmented reality, we overlay graphics on top of an object in real time. In order to do that, we need to know the location and orientation of the camera, and we need to do it quickly. This is where pose estimation becomes very important. If you don't track the pose correctly, the overlaid graphics will look unnatural.

Consider the following image:

The arrow indiactes that the surface is normal. Let's say the object changes its orientation:

Now, even though the location is the same, the orientation has changed. We need to have this information so that the overlaid graphics look natural. We need to make sure that the graphic is aligned with this orientation and position.

How to track planar objects

Now that you understand what pose estimation is, let's see how you can use it to track planar objects. Let's consider the following planar object:

Now, if we extract feature points from this image, we will see something like this:

Let's tilt the cardboard box:

As we can see, the cardboard box is tilted in this image. Now, if we want to make sure our virtual object is overlaid on top of this surface, we need to gather this planar tilt information. One way to do this is by using the relative positions of the feature points. If we extract the feature points from the preceding image, it will look like this:

As you can see, the feature points got closer horizontally on the far end of the plane as compared to the ones on the near end:

So, we can utilize this information to extract the orientation information from the image. If you remember, we discussed perspective transformation in detail when we were discussing geometric transformations, as well as panoramic imaging. All we need to do is use those two sets of points and extract the homography matrix. This homography matrix will tell us how the cardboard box turned.

Consider the following image:

First, we will start by selecting the region of interest using the ROISelector class, and once we've done that, we will pass those coordinates to PoseEstimator:

```
class ROISelector(object):
    def __init__(self, win_name, init_frame, callback_func):
        self.callback_func = callback_func
        self.selected_rect = None
        self.drag_start = None
        self.tracking_state = 0
        event_params = {"frame": init_frame}
        cv2.namedWindow(win_name)
        cv2.setMouseCallback(win_name, self.mouse_event, event_params)

    def mouse_event(self, event, x, y, flags, param):
        x, y = np.int16([x, y])

        # Detecting the mouse button down event
        if event == cv2.EVENT_LBUTTONDOWN:
            self.drag_start = (x, y)
            self.tracking_state = 0
```

```
        if self.drag_start:
            if event == cv2.EVENT_MOUSEMOVE:
                h, w = param["frame"].shape[:2]
                xo, yo = self.drag_start
                x0, y0 = np.maximum(0, np.minimum([xo, yo], [x, y]))
                x1, y1 = np.minimum([w, h], np.maximum([xo, yo], [x, y]))
                self.selected_rect = None

                if x1-x0 > 0 and y1-y0 > 0:
                    self.selected_rect = (x0, y0, x1, y1)

            elif event == cv2.EVENT_LBUTTONUP:
                self.drag_start = None
                if self.selected_rect is not None:
                    self.callback_func(self.selected_rect)
                    self.selected_rect = None
                    self.tracking_state = 1

    def draw_rect(self, img, rect):
        if not rect: return False
        x_start, y_start, x_end, y_end = rect
        cv2.rectangle(img, (x_start, y_start), (x_end, y_end), (0, 255, 0),
2)
        return True
```

In the following image, the region of interest the green rectangle:

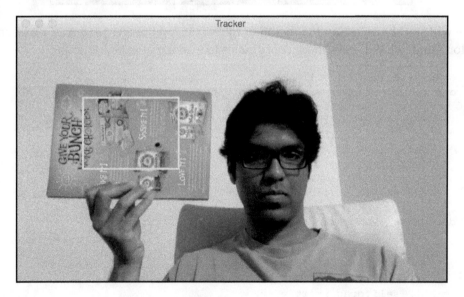

We then extract feature points from this region of interest. Since we are tracking planar objects, the algorithm assumes that this region of interest is a plane. That's obvious, but it's better to state it explicitly! So make sure you have a cardboard box in your hand when you select this region of interest. Also, it'll be better if the cardboard box has a bunch of patterns and distinctive points so that it's easy to detect and track the feature points on it.

The `PoseEstimator` class will receive areas of interest from its method, `add_target()`, and will extract those feature points from them, which will allow us to track object movements:

```python
class PoseEstimator(object):
    def __init__(self):
        # Use locality sensitive hashing algorithm
        flann_params = dict(algorithm = 6, table_number = 6, key_size = 12,
multi_probe_level = 1)

        self.min_matches = 10
        self.cur_target = namedtuple('Current', 'image, rect, keypoints,
descriptors, data')
        self.tracked_target = namedtuple('Tracked', 'target, points_prev,
points_cur, H, quad')

        self.feature_detector = cv2.ORB_create()
        self.feature_detector.setMaxFeatures(1000)
        self.feature_matcher = cv2.FlannBasedMatcher(flann_params, {})
        self.tracking_targets = []

    # Function to add a new target for tracking
    def add_target(self, image, rect, data=None):
        x_start, y_start, x_end, y_end = rect
        keypoints, descriptors = [], []
        for keypoint, descriptor in zip(*self.detect_features(image)):
            x, y = keypoint.pt
            if x_start <= x <= x_end and y_start <= y <= y_end:
                keypoints.append(keypoint)
                descriptors.append(descriptor)

        descriptors = np.array(descriptors, dtype='uint8')
        self.feature_matcher.add([descriptors])
        target = self.cur_target(image=image, rect=rect,
keypoints=keypoints, descriptors=descriptors, data=None)
        self.tracking_targets.append(target)

    # To get a list of detected objects
    def track_target(self, frame):
        self.cur_keypoints, self.cur_descriptors =
```

```
self.detect_features(frame)

        if len(self.cur_keypoints) < self.min_matches: return []
        try: matches = self.feature_matcher.knnMatch(self.cur_descriptors,
k=2)
        except Exception as e:
            print('Invalid target, please select another with features to
extract')
            return []
        matches = [match[0] for match in matches if len(match) == 2 and
match[0].distance < match[1].distance * 0.75]
        if len(matches) < self.min_matches: return []

        matches_using_index = [[] for _ in
range(len(self.tracking_targets))]
        for match in matches:
            matches_using_index[match.imgIdx].append(match)

        tracked = []
        for image_index, matches in enumerate(matches_using_index):
            if len(matches) < self.min_matches: continue

            target = self.tracking_targets[image_index]
            points_prev = [target.keypoints[m.trainIdx].pt for m in
matches]
            points_cur = [self.cur_keypoints[m.queryIdx].pt for m in
matches]
            points_prev, points_cur = np.float32((points_prev, points_cur))
            H, status = cv2.findHomography(points_prev, points_cur,
cv2.RANSAC, 3.0)
            status = status.ravel() != 0

            if status.sum() < self.min_matches: continue

            points_prev, points_cur = points_prev[status],
points_cur[status]

            x_start, y_start, x_end, y_end = target.rect
            quad = np.float32([[x_start, y_start], [x_end, y_start],
[x_end, y_end], [x_start, y_end]])
            quad = cv2.perspectiveTransform(quad.reshape(1, -1, 2),
H).reshape(-1, 2)
            track = self.tracked_target(target=target,
points_prev=points_prev, points_cur=points_cur, H=H, quad=quad)
            tracked.append(track)

        tracked.sort(key = lambda x: len(x.points_prev), reverse=True)
        return tracked
```

```
    # Detect features in the selected ROIs and return the keypoints and
descriptors
    def detect_features(self, frame):
        keypoints, descriptors =
self.feature_detector.detectAndCompute(frame, None)
        if descriptors is None: descriptors = []
        return keypoints, descriptors

    # Function to clear all the existing targets
    def clear_targets(self):
        self.feature_matcher.clear()
        self.tracking_targets = []
```

Let the tracking begin! We'll move the cardboard box around to see what happens:

As you can see, the feature points are being tracked inside the region of interest. Let's hold it at an angle and see what happens:

Looks like the feature points are being tracked properly. As we can see, the overlaid rectangle is changing its orientation according to the surface of the cardboard box.

Here is the code to do this:

```
import sys
from collections import namedtuple

import cv2
import numpy as np

class VideoHandler(object):
    def __init__(self, capId, scaling_factor, win_name):
        self.cap = cv2.VideoCapture(capId)
        self.pose_tracker = PoseEstimator()
        self.win_name = win_name
        self.scaling_factor = scaling_factor

        ret, frame = self.cap.read()
        self.rect = None
        self.frame = cv2.resize(frame, None, fx=scaling_factor,
fy=scaling_factor, interpolation=cv2.INTER_AREA)
        self.roi_selector = ROISelector(win_name, self.frame,
self.set_rect)
```

```
    def set_rect(self, rect):
        self.rect = rect
        self.pose_tracker.add_target(self.frame, rect)

    def start(self):
        paused = False
        while True:
            if not paused or self.frame is None:
                ret, frame = self.cap.read()
                scaling_factor = self.scaling_factor
                frame = cv2.resize(frame, None, fx=scaling_factor,
fy=scaling_factor, interpolation=cv2.INTER_AREA)
                if not ret: break
                self.frame = frame.copy()

            img = self.frame.copy()
            if not paused and self.rect is not None:
                tracked = self.pose_tracker.track_target(self.frame)
                for item in tracked:
                    cv2.polylines(img, [np.int32(item.quad)], True, (255,
255, 255), 2)
                    for (x, y) in np.int32(item.points_cur):
                        cv2.circle(img, (x, y), 2, (255, 255, 255))

            self.roi_selector.draw_rect(img, self.rect)
            cv2.imshow(self.win_name, img)
            ch = cv2.waitKey(1)
            if ch == ord(' '): paused = not paused
            if ch == ord('c'): self.pose_tracker.clear_targets()
            if ch == 27: break

if __name__ == '__main__':
    VideoHandler(0, 0.8, 'Tracker').start()
```

What happened inside the code?

To start with, we have a `PoseEstimator` class that does all the heavy lifting here. We need something to detect the features in the image and something to match the features between successive images. So we use the ORB feature detector and the Flann feature matcher for fast nearest neighbor searches within the extracted features. As you can see, we initialize the class with these parameters in the constructor.

Whenever we select a region of interest, we call the `add_target` method to add that to our list of tracking targets. This method just extracts the features from that region of interest and stores them in one of the class variables. Now that we have a target, we are ready to track it!

The `track_target` method handles all the tracking. We take the current frame and extract all the keypoints. However, we are not really interested in all the keypoints in the current frame of the video. We just want the keypoints that belong to our target object. So now our job is to find the closest keypoints in the current frame.

We now have a set of keypoints in the current frame and we have another set of keypoints from our target object in the previous frame. The next step is to extract the homography matrix from these matching points. This homography matrix tells us how to transform the overlaid rectangle so that it's aligned with the surface of the cardboard box. We just need to take this homography matrix and apply it to the overlaid rectangle to obtain the new positions of all the cardboard box's points.

How to augment our reality

Now that we know how to track planar objects, let's see how to overlay 3D objects on top of the real world. The objects are 3D but the video on our screen is 2D. So, the first step here is to understand how to map those 3D objects to 2D surfaces so that they look realistic. We just need to project those 3D points onto planar surfaces.

Mapping coordinates from 3D to 2D

Once we estimate the pose, we project the points from 3D to 2D. Consider the following image:

As we can see here, the TV remote control is a 3D object but we are seeing it on a 2D plane. Now if we move it around, it will look like this:

This 3D object is still on a 2D plane. The object has moved to a different location and the distance from the camera has changed as well. How do we compute these coordinates? We need a mechanism to map this 3D object onto the 2D surface. This is where 3D-to-2D projection becomes really important.

We just need to estimate the initial camera pose to start with. Now, let's assume that the intrinsic parameters of the camera are already known. So, we can just use the `solvePnP` function in OpenCV to estimate the camera's pose. This function is used to estimate the object's pose using a set of points as seen in the following code. You can read more about it at http://docs.opencv.org/modules/calib3d/doc/camera_calibration_and_3d_ reconstruction.html#bool:

```
solvePnP(InputArray objectPoints, InputArray imagePoints, InputArray
cameraMatrix, InputArray distCoeffs, OutputArray rvec, OutputArray tvec,
bool useExtrinsicGuess, int flags)
```

Once we do this, we need to project these points onto a 2D plane. We use the OpenCV `projectPoints` function to do this. This function calculates the projections of those 3D points onto the 2D plane.

How to overlay 3D objects on a video

Now that we have all the different blocks, we are ready to build the final system. Let's say we want to overlay a pyramid on top of our cardboard box, as shown here:

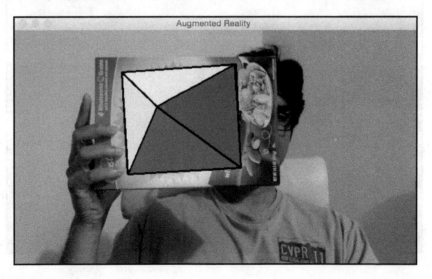

Let's tilt the cardboard box to see what happens:

Looks like the pyramid is following the surface. Let's add a second target:

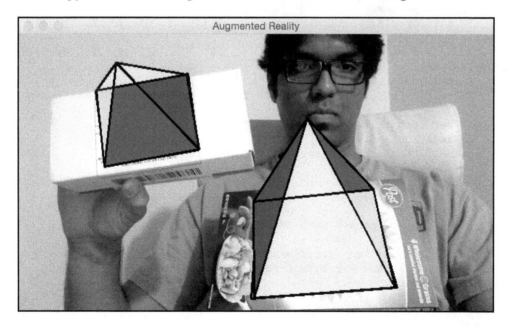

You can keep adding more targets and all those pyramids will be tracked nicely. Let's see how to do this using OpenCV Python. Make sure to save the previous file as `pose_estimation.py` because we will be importing a couple of classes from there:

```python
import cv2
import numpy as np

from pose_estimation import PoseEstimator, ROISelector

class Tracker(object):
    def __init__(self, capId, scaling_factor, win_name):
        self.cap = cv2.VideoCapture(capId)
        self.rect = None
        self.win_name = win_name
        self.scaling_factor = scaling_factor
        self.tracker = PoseEstimator()

        ret, frame = self.cap.read()
        self.rect = None
        self.frame = cv2.resize(frame, None, fx=scaling_factor,
fy=scaling_factor, interpolation=cv2.INTER_AREA)

        self.roi_selector = ROISelector(win_name, self.frame,
self.set_rect)
        self.overlay_vertices = np.float32([[0, 0, 0], [0, 1, 0], [1, 1,
0], [1, 0, 0], [0.5, 0.5, 4]])
        self.overlay_edges = [(0, 1), (1, 2), (2, 3), (3, 0), (0,4), (1,4),
(2,4), (3,4)]
        self.color_base = (0, 255, 0)
        self.color_lines = (0, 0, 0)

    def set_rect(self, rect):
        self.rect = rect
        self.tracker.add_target(self.frame, rect)

    def start(self):
        paused = False
        while True:
            if not paused or self.frame is None:
                ret, frame = self.cap.read()
                scaling_factor = self.scaling_factor
                frame = cv2.resize(frame, None, fx=scaling_factor,
fy=scaling_factor, \
                    interpolation=cv2.INTER_AREA)
                if not ret: break

                self.frame = frame.copy()
```

```
        img = self.frame.copy()
        if not paused:
            tracked = self.tracker.track_target(self.frame)
            for item in tracked:
                cv2.polylines(img, [np.int32(item.quad)],
                 True, self.color_lines, 2)
                for (x, y) in np.int32(item.points_cur):
                    cv2.circle(img, (x, y), 2,
                     self.color_lines)

                self.overlay_graphics(img, item)

        self.roi_selector.draw_rect(img, self.rect)
        cv2.imshow(self.win_name, img)
        ch = cv2.waitKey(1)
        if ch == ord(' '): self.paused = not self.paused
        if ch == ord('c'): self.tracker.clear_targets()
        if ch == 27: break

    def overlay_graphics(self, img, tracked):
        x_start, y_start, x_end, y_end = tracked.target.rect
        quad_3d = np.float32([[x_start, y_start, 0], [x_end,
         y_start, 0],
                    [x_end, y_end, 0], [x_start, y_end, 0]])
        h, w = img.shape[:2]
        K = np.float64([[w, 0, 0.5*(w-1)],
                    [0, w, 0.5*(h-1)],
                    [0, 0, 1.0]])
        dist_coef = np.zeros(4)
        ret, rvec, tvec = cv2.solvePnP(objectPoints=quad_3d,
imagePoints=tracked.quad,
                               cameraMatrix=K,
distCoeffs=dist_coef)
        verts = self.overlay_vertices * \
            [(x_end-x_start), (y_end-y_start), -(x_end-x_start)*0.3] +
(x_start, y_start, 0)
        verts = cv2.projectPoints(verts, rvec, tvec, cameraMatrix=K,
distCoeffs=dist_coef)[0].reshape(-1, 2)

        verts_floor = np.int32(verts).reshape(-1,2)
        cv2.drawContours(img, contours=[verts_floor[:4]], contourIdx=-1,
color=self.color_base, thickness=-3)
        cv2.drawContours(img, contours=[np.vstack((verts_floor[:2],
verts_floor[4:5]))], contourIdx=-1, color=(0,255,0), thickness=-3)
        cv2.drawContours(img, contours=[np.vstack((verts_floor[1:3],
verts_floor[4:5]))], contourIdx=-1, color=(255,0,0), thickness=-3)
        cv2.drawContours(img, contours=[np.vstack((verts_floor[2:4],
verts_floor[4:5]))], contourIdx=-1, color=(0,0,150), thickness=-3)
```

```
        cv2.drawContours(img, contours=[np.vstack((verts_floor[3:4],
verts_floor[0:1], verts_floor[4:5]))], contourIdx=-1, color=(255,255,0),
thickness=-3)

        for i, j in self.overlay_edges:
            (x_start, y_start), (x_end, y_end) = verts[i], verts[j]
            cv2.line(img, (int(x_start), int(y_start)), (int(x_end),
int(y_end)), self.color_lines, 2)

if __name__ == '__main__':
    Tracker(0, 0.8, 'Augmented Reality').start()
```

Let's look at the code

The `Tracker` class is used to perform all the computations here. We initialize the class with the pyramid structure that is defined using edges and vertices. The logic that we use to track the surface is the same as we discussed earlier because we are using the same class. We just need to use `solvePnP` and `projectPoints` to map the 3D pyramid to the 2D surface.

Let's add some movements

Now that we know how to add a virtual pyramid, let's see if we can add some movements. Let's see how we can dynamically change the height of the pyramid. When you start, the pyramid will look like this:

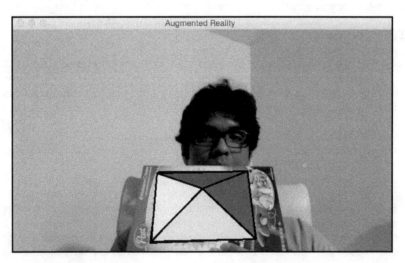

If you wait for some time, the pyramid gets taller and will look like this:

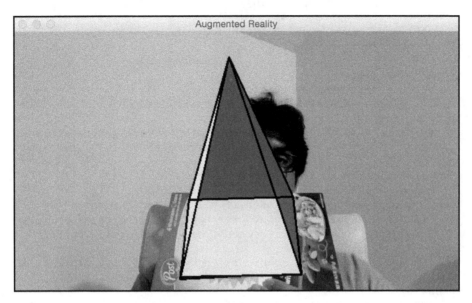

Let's see how to do it in OpenCV Python. Inside the augmented reality code that we just discussed, add the following snippet at the end of the __init__ method in the `Tracker` class:

```
self.overlay_vertices = np.float32([[0, 0, 0], [0, 1, 0], [1, 1, 0], [1, 0,
0], [0.5, 0.5, 4]])
self.overlay_edges = [(0, 1), (1, 2), (2, 3), (3, 0),
            (0,4), (1,4), (2,4), (3,4)]
self.color_base = (0, 255, 0)
self.color_lines = (0, 0, 0)

self.graphics_counter = 0
self.time_counter = 0
```

Now that we have the structure, we need to add the code to dynamically change the height. Replace the `overlay_graphics()` method with the following method:

```
def overlay_graphics(self, img, tracked):
    x_start, y_start, x_end, y_end = tracked.target.rect
    quad_3d = np.float32([[x_start, y_start, 0], [x_end,
    y_start, 0],
                [x_end, y_end, 0], [x_start, y_end, 0]])
    h, w = img.shape[:2]
    K = np.float64([[w, 0, 0.5*(w-1)],
```

```
                    [0, w, 0.5*(h-1)],
                    [0, 0, 1.0]])
        dist_coef = np.zeros(4)
        ret, rvec, tvec = cv2.solvePnP(objectPoints=quad_3d,
imagePoints=tracked.quad,
                                    cameraMatrix=K,
distCoeffs=dist_coef)
        verts = self.overlay_vertices * \
            [(x_end-x_start), (y_end-y_start), -(x_end-x_start)*0.3] +
(x_start, y_start, 0)
        verts = cv2.projectPoints(verts, rvec, tvec, cameraMatrix=K,
                            distCoeffs=dist_coef)[0].reshape(-1, 2)

        verts_floor = np.int32(verts).reshape(-1,2)
        cv2.drawContours(img, contours=[verts_floor[:4]],
            contourIdx=-1, color=self.color_base, thickness=-3)
        cv2.drawContours(img, contours=[np.vstack((verts_floor[:2],
            verts_floor[4:5]))], contourIdx=-1, color=(0,255,0),
thickness=-3)
        cv2.drawContours(img, contours=[np.vstack((verts_floor[1:3],
            verts_floor[4:5]))], contourIdx=-1, color=(255,0,0),
thickness=-3)
        cv2.drawContours(img, contours=[np.vstack((verts_floor[2:4],
            verts_floor[4:5]))], contourIdx=-1, color=(0,0,150),
thickness=-3)
        cv2.drawContours(img, contours=[np.vstack((verts_floor[3:4],
            verts_floor[0:1], verts_floor[4:5]))], contourIdx=-1,
color=(255,255,0),thickness=-3)

        for i, j in self.overlay_edges:
            (x_start, y_start), (x_end, y_end) = verts[i], verts[j]
            cv2.line(img, (int(x_start), int(y_start)), (int(x_end),
int(y_end)),
                self.color_lines, 2)
```

Now that we know how to change the height, let's go ahead and make the pyramid dance for us. We can make the tip of the pyramid oscillate periodically. So when you start, it will look like this:

If you wait for some time, it will look like this:

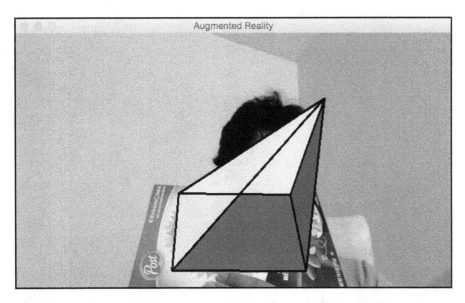

You can look at `augmented_reality_motion.py` for the implementation details.

In our next experiment, we will make the whole pyramid move around the region of interest. We can make it move in any way we want. Let's start by adding linear diagonal movement around our selected region of interest. When you start, it will look like this:

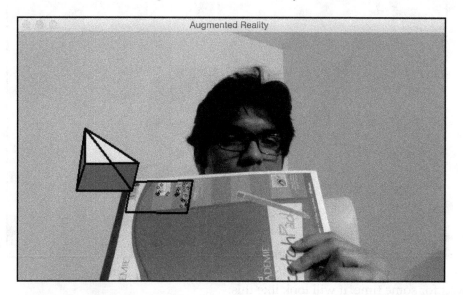

After some time, it will look like this:

Refer to `augmented_reality_dancing.py` to see how to change the `overlay_graphics()` method to make it dance. Let's see if we can make the pyramid go around in circles around our region of interest. When you start, it will look like this:

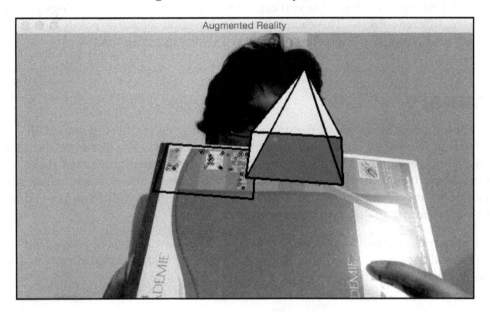

After some time, it will move to a new position:

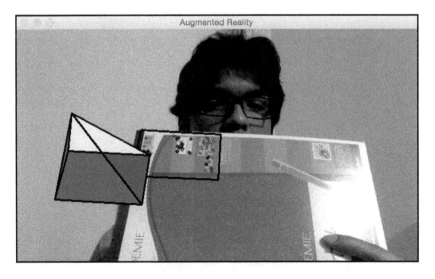

You can refer to `augmented_reality_circular_motion.py` to see how to make this happen. You can make it do anything you want. You just need to come up with the right mathematical formula and the pyramid will literally dance to your tune! You can also try out other virtual objects to see what you can do with it. There are a lot of things you can do with a lot of different objects. These examples provide good reference points, on top of which you can build many interesting augmented reality applications.

Summary

In this chapter, you learned about the premise of augmented reality and gained an understanding of what an augmented reality system looks like. We discussed the geometric transformations required for augmented reality. You also learned how to use those transformations to estimate the camera pose, and you learned how to track planar objects. We discussed how we can add virtual objects on top of the real world. You learned how to modify virtual objects in different ways to add cool effects.

In the next chapter, we will learn how to apply machine learning techniques, along with artificial neural networks, which will help us to enhance the knowledge already acquired in Chapter 9, *Object Recognition*.

11
Machine Learning by an Artificial Neural Network

In this chapter, you will learn how to build an ANN and train it to perform image classification and object recognition. ANNs are one of the subsets of Machine Learning, and we will talk particularly about MLP networks, which are the most common type of neural networks on pattern recognition scopes.

By the end of this chapter, we will have cover the following:

- The difference between **machine learning** (**ML**) and **artificial neural network** (**ANN**)
- **Multi-layer perceptrons** (**MLP**) networks
- How to define and implement an MLP network
- Evaluate and improve our ANN
- How to recognize objects in images using a trained ANN

Machine learning (ML) versus artificial neural network (ANN)

As mentioned earlier, an ANN is a subset of ML. ANNs are inspired by human understanding; they work as our brain does, composed of different interconnected layers of neurons, where each of them receives information from previous one, processes it, and sends it to the next one until the final output is received. This output could be from a labeled output in the case of supervised learning or certain criteria matching in the case of unsupervised learning.

What are the peculiarities of an ANN? Machine learning is defined as the area in computer science that focuses on trying to find patterns within data sets, and ANN is more oriented toward simulating how human brains are connected to make that work, splitting pattern detection across several layers/nodes that we will call neurons.

Meanwhile, other machine learning algorithms such as **support vector machine (SVM)** are more popular and established on the object pattern recognition and classification. SVM has one of the best accuracies in machine learning algorithms. ANN has a larger set of applications that are able to detect patterns on most any kind of data structure (SVM works mostly with feature vectors) and can be more parameterized to achieve different goals within the same implementation.

Moreover, another advantage of ANN over other ML strategies such as SVM is that ANN is a probabilistic classifier allowing multi-class classification. This means that it can detect more than a single object within an image; whereas on the flip side, SVM is a non-probabilistic binary classifier.

When can an ANN be useful? Imagine we had implemented an object recognizer trained to recognize backpacks and footwear, and then we have the following image:

We run our feature detector on it and we obtain a result as shown:

As you can see from the previous image, our feature detector algorithm obtained feature vectors from the *backpack* and *footwear* of the girl. So if we run our SVM classifier from Chapter 9, *Object Recognition*, on this image, due to the linear classifier implementation, it would rather detect only the *backpack* even if the image contains footwear as well.

 SVM might also perform a non-linear classification using something called a **kernel trick** and implicitly map the inputs into high-dimensional feature spaces.

How does ANN work?

In this section, we will see which are the elements taking part in an ANN-MLP. First, we will represent a regular ANN-MLP shape with one layer each of input, output, and hidden, and how the information flows across them:

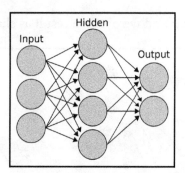

An MLP network is formed by at least three layers:

- **Input layer**: Every MLP always has one of these layers. It is a passive layer, which means that it does not modify the data. It receives information from the outside world and sends it out to the network. The number of nodes (neurons) in this layer will depend on the amount of features or descriptive information we want to extract from the images. For example, in case of using feature vectors, there will be one node for each of the columns within the vector.
- **Hidden layers**: This layer is where all the groundwork happens. It transforms the inputs into something that the output layer or another hidden layer can use (there can be more than one). This layer works as a black box, sensing patterns within received inputs and evaluating the weights on each of them. Its behavior will be defined by the equation provided by its activation function.

- **Output layer**: This layer will also always exist, but the number of nodes in this case will be defined by the chosen neural network. This layer might have three neurons. The output layer may be built by a single node (linear regression), that is, we want to know whether an image has a backpack or not. But in the case of multi-class classification, this layer will contain several nodes, one per object, that we can identify. Each node will produce a value, by default in the range of [-1,1], defining the probability of the object to be there or not and allowing multi-class detection on a single input image.

Let's say we want to build a three-layered neural network with one of each: input, hidden, and output. The number of nodes in the input layer will be determined by the dimensionality of our data. The number of nodes in the output layer will be defined by the number of models we have. Regarding the hidden layer, the number of nodes or even layers will be determined by the complexity of the problem and the accuracy we want to add into the network. A high dimensionality will improve the accuracy on the results, but it will also add to the computational cost. Another decision to be taken for the hidden layer is the use of an activation function, which allows us to fit nonlinear hypotheses and obtain better pattern detection depending of the data provided. A common choice for activation functions is the `Sigmoid` function, which is the one used by default where outputs are evaluated in terms of probabilities, but there are others choices too such as **tanh** or **ReLUs**.

On a deeper look at each neuron with a hidden layer, we can say that all of them behave in a similar way. Values are retrieved from the previous layer (input nodes), summed up with certain weights (individual for each neuron) plus the bias term. The sum is transformed using the activation function, *f*, that may also be different for different neurons, as represented in the following image:

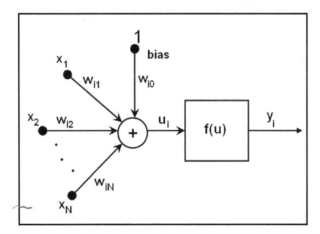

How to define multi-layer perceptrons (MLP)

MLP is a branch of ANNs widely used in pattern recognition because of its ability of identify patterns within noisy or unexpected environments. MLP can be used to implement supervised and unsupervised learning (both of them were discussed Chapter 9, *Object Recognition*). In addition to that, MLP can also be used to implement another kind of learning such as reinforcement learning inspired by behavioral psychology, where the network learning is adjusted using reward/punishment actions.

Defining an ANN-MLP consist of deciding the structure of the layers that will compose our net, and how many nodes will be in each of them. Firstly, we need to decide what the goal of our network is. For instance, we could implement an object recognizer, in which case, the number of nodes belonging to the output layer will be the same as the number of different objects we want to identify. Simulating the example from Chapter 9, Object Recognition, in the case of recognizing handbags, footwear, and dresses, the output layer will have three nodes, and their values will be mapped as tuples of probabilities instead of a fixed values such as *[1,0,0], [0,1,0],* and *[0,0,1]*. Therefore, it would be possible to identify more than one single class in the same image, for example, a girl with a backpack wearing slippers.

Once we have decided the outcome of our network, we should define which meaningful information of each object to recognize could be inserted into our network to be able to identify objects into unknown images. There are several approaches as a feature descriptor for the images. We could use **Histogram of Orient Gradients (HOG)**, which counts occurrences of gradient orientation in localized portions of an image, or *Color Histogram*, which represents the distribution of colors in the image, or we could also extract image features using dense feature detectors with SIFT or SURF algorithms. Since the number of descriptors need to be the same for every image inserted into the input layer, we will use the *Bag of Words* strategy, collecting all sets of descriptors into a single histogram of visual words as we did in Chapter 9, *Object Recognition*, for the use of the SVM recognizer. The histogram would look as shown here, where each of the bar values will be linked to one node within the input layer:

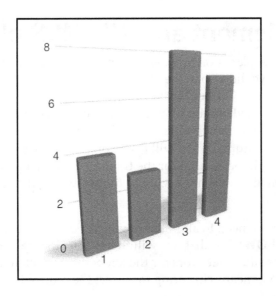

At last, we come to hidden layers. This layer does not have a strictly defined structure, thus it will be a complex decision. There is a large discussion among different researchers on how to decide the number of hidden layers and the number of nodes in them. All of them rely on the complexity of the problem to resolve and finding a balance between performance and accuracy—more nodes/layers will have more accuracy but low performance. Also, a large number of nodes might cause and over-fitted network cause not only lower performance but also lower accuracy. In the case of a simple object recognizer with only three models, it does not require more than a single hidden layer, and regarding the number of nodes in there, we could take, for instance, Heaton research (`http://www.heatonresearch.com/2017/06/01/hidden-layers.html`), which sets the following rules:

- The number of hidden neurons should be between the size of the input layer and the size of the output layer
- The number of hidden neurons should be two-thirds of the size of the input layer plus the size of the output layer
- The number of hidden neurons should be less than twice the size of the input layer

How to implement an ANN-MLP classifier?

After all that theoretical explanation on how to implement an ANN, we will implement it ourself. For that, and as we did also in the SVM classifier, we will download the training images from the same source **Caltech256**, `http://www.vision.caltech.edu/Image_Datasets/Caltech256`. We will start with a few items, easily extendable to many other, creating a folder, `images`, with a subfolder for each of the categories that we will classify: `dresses`, `footwear`, and `bagpack`. We will take a bunch of images for each of them; around 20-25 images should be enough for the training, and on top of that we will include another set of sample images, which we will use for evaluating the accuracy of our network after the training.

As we discussed earlier, we need to align the number of descriptors for each of the images using a **Bag of Words** (**BOW**). For that, we will first extract the feature vectors for each of the images using dense feature detectors for the keypoints of each image feed and then forward the vectors into k-means clustering to extract the centroids, which will help us to finally obtain the BOW.

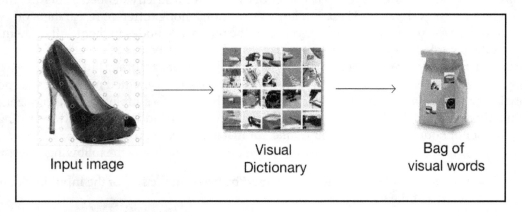

Input image   Visual Dictionary   Bag of visual words

As you can recognize from the previous image, it was the same process we implemented during the SVM classifier. In order to save some time and code, we will take advantage of the `create_features.py` file created earlier to extract all the feature descriptors we will use as the input of our MLP network.

By running the following command, we will obtain every map file required for the next step:

```
$ python create_features.py --samples bag images/bagpack/ --samples dress
images/dress/ --samples footwear images/footwear/ --codebook-file
models/codebook.pkl --feature-map-file models/feature_map.pkl
```

Within the `feature_map.pkl` file, we have a vector of features of each of the images which will take part during the training phase. First, we will create a class for our ANN classifier, where we will set the sizes of our network layers:

```
from sklearn import preprocessing
import numpy as np
import cv2
import random

class ClassifierANN(object):
    def __init__(self, feature_vector_size, label_words):
        self.ann = cv2.ml.ANN_MLP_create()
        self.label_words = label_words
        # Number of centroids used to build the feature vectors
        input_size = feature_vector_size
        # Number of models to recongnize
        output_size = len(label_words)
        # Applying Heaton rules
        hidden_size = (input_size * (2/3)) + output_size
        nn_config = np.array([input_size, hidden_size, output_size],
dtype=np.uint8)
        self.ann.setLayerSizes(np.array(nn_config))
        # Symmetrical Sigmoid as activation function
        self.ann.setActivationFunction(cv2.ml.ANN_MLP_SIGMOID_SYM, 2, 1)
        # Map models as tuples of probabilities
        self.le = preprocessing.LabelBinarizer()
        self.le.fit(label_words) # Label words are ['dress', 'footwear',
'backpack']
```

As output, we decided to implement a tuple of probabilities with binary numbers [0,0,1], [0,1,0], [1,0,0] aiming that way the option to obtain multi-class detection. As the activation function symmetrical Sigmoid (`NN_MLP_SIGMOID_SYM`), which is the default choice for MLP, where outputs will be in the range of [-1,1]. This way, the output generated by our network will define probabilities instead of categorical outcomes, being able to identify two or three objects within the same sample image.

For the training process, we will split our data set into two different sets: training and testing. We will define a ratio for it (usually, most of the examples recommend using 75% as the training set, but it could be adjusted until best accuracy is obtained) and randomize the selection of the items to prevent bias. How does that work?

```
class ClassifierANN(object):
    ...
    def train(self, training_set):
        label_words = [ item['label'] for item in training_set]
        dim_size = training_set[0]['feature_vector'].shape[1]
```

```
        train_samples = np.asarray(
            [np.reshape(x['feature_vector'], (dim_size,)) for x in
training_set]
        )
        # Convert item labels into encoded binary tuples
        train_response = np.array(self.le.transform(label_words),
dtype=np.float32)
        self.ann.train(np.array(train_samples,
            dtype=np.float32),cv2.ml.ROW_SAMPLE,
            np.array(train_response, dtype=np.float32)
        )
```

In this case, we had used the same weights for each of the nodes for our input layer (default behavior), but we could have specified them giving more weights to the columns within feature vector with more significant information.

Evaluate a trained network

To evaluate the robustness and accuracy of our trained MLP network, we will calculate the confusion matrix (also known as error matrix). This matrix will describe the performance of our classification model. Each row of the confusion matrix represents the instances in a predicted class, while each column represents the instances in an actual class (or vice versa). To fill up the matrix, we will use our testing set to evaluate it:

```
from collections import OrderedDict

def init_confusion_matrix(self, label_words):
    confusion_matrix = OrderedDict()
    for label in label_words:
        confusion_matrix[label] = OrderedDict()
        for label2 in label_words: confusion_matrix[label][label2] = 0
    return confusion_matrix

# Chooses the class with the greatest value, only one, in the
tuple(encoded_word)
def classify(self, encoded_word, threshold=0.5):
    models = self.le.inverse_transform(np.asarray([encoded_word]),
threshold)
    return models[0]

# Calculate the confusion matrix from given testing data set
def get_confusion_matrix(self, testing_set):
    label_words = [item['label'] for item in testing_set]
    dim_size = testing_set[0]['feature_vector'].shape[1]
    test_samples = np.asarray(
```

```
        [np.reshape(x['feature_vector'], (dim_size,)) for x in testing_set]
    )
    expected_outputs = np.array(self.le.transform(label_words),
dtype=np.float32)
    confusion_matrix = self._init_confusion_matrix(label_words)
    retval, test_outputs = self.ann.predict(test_samples)
    for expected_output, test_output in zip(expected_outputs,
test_outputs):
        expected_model = self.classify(expected_output)
        predicted_model = self.classify(test_output)
        confusion_matrix[expected_model][predicted_model] += 1
    return confusion_matrix
```

As the sample confusion matrix, and considering a testing set of 30 elements, we might have obtained the following results:

	footwear	backpack	dress
footwear	8	2	0
backpack	2	7	1
dress	2	2	6

Considering the previous matrix, we could calculate the accuracy of our trained network by the following formula:

$$ACC = \frac{TP + TN}{TP + TN + FP + FN}$$

In this formula, we have represented **True Positives (TP)**, **True Negatives** (TN), **False Positives (FP)**, and **False Negatives (FN)**. In the case of footwear, we could say that its accuracy was 80%.

$$\frac{8 + 16}{8 + 16 + 4 + 2} = 0.8$$

The implementation code for the preceding formula is as follows:

```
def calculate_accuracy(confusion_matrix):
    acc_models = OrderedDict()
    for model in confusion_matrix.keys():
        acc_models[model] = {'TP':0, 'TN':0, 'FP':0, 'FN': 0}
    for expected_model, predicted_models in confusion_matrix.items():
        for predicted_model, value in predicted_models.items():
            if predicted_model == expected_model:
                acc_models[expected_model]['TP'] += value
                acc_models[predicted_model]['TN'] += value
```

```
            else:
                acc_models[expected_model]['FN'] += value
                acc_models[predicted_model]['FP'] += value


    for model, rep in acc_models.items():
        acc =
(rep['TP']+rep['TN'])/(rep['TP']+rep['TN']+rep['FN']+rep['FP'])
        print('%s \t %f' % (model,acc))
```

Collecting every code block from this section, we have already implemented the `ClassifierANN` class ready for its use:

```
##############
# training.py
##############

import pickle

def build_arg_parser():
    parser = argparse.ArgumentParser(description='Creates features for
given images')
    parser.add_argument("--feature-map-file", dest="feature_map_file",
required=True,
        help="Input pickle file containing the feature map")
    parser.add_argument("--training-set", dest="training_set",
required=True,
        help="Percentage taken for training. ie 0.75")
    parser.add_argument("--ann-file", dest="ann_file", required=False,
        help="Output file where ANN will be stored")
    parser.add_argument("--le-file", dest="le_file", required=False,
                        help="Output file where LabelEncoder class will be
stored")


if __name__ == '__main__':
    args = build_arg_parser().parse_args()

    # Load the Feature Map
    with open(args.feature_map_file, 'rb') as f:
        feature_map = pickle.load(f)

    training_set, testing_set = split_feature_map(feature_map,
float(args.training_set))
    label_words = np.unique([item['label'] for item in training_set])
    cnn = ClassifierANN(len(feature_map[0]['feature_vector'][0]),
label_words)
```

```
cnn.train(training_set)
print("===== Confusion Matrix =====")
confusion_matrix = cnn.get_confusion_matrix(testing_set)
print(confusion_matrix)
print("===== ANN Accuracy =====")
print_accuracy(confusion_matrix)

if 'ann_file' in args and 'le_file' in args:
    print("===== Saving ANN =====")
    with open(args.ann_file, 'wb') as f:
        cnn.ann.save(args.ann_file)
    with open(args.le_file, 'wb') as f:
        pickle.dump(cnn.le, f)
    print('Saved in: ', args.ann_file)
```

As you may have noticed, we have saved our ANN into two separate files, because
ANN_MLP classes have their own save and load methods. We need to save label_words
used to train our network. Pickle provides to us the functionalities to serialize and de-
serialize object structure and save and load them from disk, with the exception of some
structure like ann which has its own implementation for it.

Run the following command to obtain model files. The confusion matrix and accuracy
probabilities will be displayed along with it:

> **$ python training.py --feature-map-file models/feature_map.pkl --training-set 0.8 --ann-file models/ann.yaml --le-file models/le.pkl**

To obtain a better-trained network, we can repeat the previous command
as many times as we desire until good accuracy results are obtained. This
happens because the training and testing sets are taken randomly, so we
should retain the one with the better outcome.

Classifying images

To implement our ANN classifier, we will need to reuse the method of the FeatureExtractor
class from the create_feature.py file in Chapter 9, *Object Recognition*, which will allow
us to calculate the feature vectors from the images we want to evaluate:

```
class FeatureExtractor(object):
    def get_feature_vector(self, img, kmeans, centroids):
        return Quantizer().get_feature_vector(img, kmeans, centroids)
```

Consider the inclusion of the `create_feature` file in the same folder. Now, we are ready to implement the classifier:

```python
##############
# classify_data.py
##############

import argparse
import _pickle as pickle

import cv2
import numpy as np

import create_features as cf

# Classifying an image
class ImageClassifier(object):
    def __init__(self, ann_file, le_file, codebook_file):
        with open(ann_file, 'rb') as f:
            self.ann = cv2.ml.ANN_MLP_load(ann_file)
        with open(le_file, 'rb') as f:
            self.le = pickle.load(f)

        # Load the codebook
        with open(codebook_file, 'rb') as f:
            self.kmeans, self.centroids = pickle.load(f)

    def classify(self, encoded_word, threshold=None):
        models = self.le.inverse_transform(np.asarray(encoded_word),
threshold)
        return models[0]

    # Method to get the output image tag
    def getImageTag(self, img):
        # Resize the input image
        img = cf.resize_to_size(img)
        # Extract the feature vector
        feature_vector = cf.FeatureExtractor().get_feature_vector(img,
self.kmeans, self.centroids)
        # Classify the feature vector and get the output tag
        retval, image_tag = self.ann.predict(feature_vector)
        return self.classify(image_tag)


def build_arg_parser():
    parser = argparse.ArgumentParser(
        description='Extracts features from each line and classifies the
```

```
data')
    parser.add_argument("--input-image", dest="input_image", required=True,
        help="Input image to be classified")
    parser.add_argument("--codebook-file", dest="codebook_file",
required=True,
        help="File containing the codebook")
    parser.add_argument("--ann-file", dest="ann_file", required=True,
        help="File containing trained ANN")
    parser.add_argument("--le-file", dest="le_file", required=True,
        help="File containing LabelEncoder class")
    return parser

if __name__=='__main__':
    args = build_arg_parser().parse_args()
    codebook_file = args.codebook_file
    input_image = cv2.imread(args.input_image)

    tag = ImageClassifier(args.ann_file, args.le_file,
codebook_file).getImageTag(input_image)
    print("Output class:", tag)
```

Run the following command to classify the images:

```
$ python classify_data.py --codebook-file models/codebook.pkl --ann-file
models/ann.yaml --le-file models/le.pkl --input-image ./images/test.png
```

Summary

In this chapter, you learned the concept of ANN. You also learned that one of its uses within the field of object recognition is the implementation of MLP, including the advantages and disadvantages of MLP against other machine learning strategies, such as SVM. Regarding ANN-MLP, you learned which layers form its structure and how to define and implement them to build an image classifier and then learned how to evaluate an MLP, training its robustness and accuracy. And in the last section, we implemented an example of an MLP to detect an object in an unknown image.

Remember that the world of computer vision is filled with endless possibilities! This book is designed to teach you the necessary skills to get started on a wide variety of projects. Now it's up to you and your imagination to use the skills you have acquired here to build something unique and interesting.

Other Books You May Enjoy

If you enjoyed this book, you may be interested in these other books by Packt:

OpenCV 3 Computer Vision Application Programming Cookbook - Third Edition
Robert Laganiere

ISBN: 978-1-78646-971-7

- Install and create a program using the OpenCV library
- Process an image by manipulating its pixels
- Analyze an image using histograms
- Segment images into homogenous regions and extract meaningful objects
- Apply image filters to enhance image content
- Exploit the image geometry in order to relay different views of a pictured scene
- Calibrate the camera from different image observations
- Detect people and objects in images using machine learning techniques
- Reconstruct a 3D scene from images

Mastering OpenCV 3 - Second Edition

Daniel Lélis Baggio, Shervin Emami, David Millán Escrivá, Khvedchenia Ievgen, Jason Saragih, Roy Shilkrot

ISBN: 978-1-78439-030-3

- Execute basic image processing operations and cartoonify an image
- Build an OpenCV project natively with Raspberry Pi and cross-compile it for Raspberry Pi.text
- Extend the natural feature tracking algorithm to support the tracking of multiple image targets on a video
- Use OpenCV 3's new 3D visualization framework to illustrate the 3D scene geometry
- Create an application for Automatic Number Plate Recognition (ANPR) using a support vector machine and Artificial Neural Networks
- Train and predict pattern-recognition algorithms to decide whether an image is a number plate
- Use POSIT for the six degrees of freedom head pose
- Train a face recognition database using deep learning and recognize faces from that database

Leave a review - let other readers know what you think

Please share your thoughts on this book with others by leaving a review on the site that you bought it from. If you purchased the book from Amazon, please leave us an honest review on this book's Amazon page. This is vital so that other potential readers can see and use your unbiased opinion to make purchasing decisions, we can understand what our customers think about our products, and our authors can see your feedback on the title that they have worked with Packt to create. It will only take a few minutes of your time, but is valuable to other potential customers, our authors, and Packt. Thank you!

Index

features
    tracking 106
frame
    differentiating 155, 157

G

Gaussian Mixture Markov Random Field (GMMRF)
    reference 151
geometric transformations
    camera-to-image 205
    object-to-scene 205
    scene-to-camera 205
GrabCut 148
graph-cuts 148

H

Haar cascades
    used, for detecting things 77
Harris Corner Detector 104
Heaton research
    reference 237
high threshold value 51
histogram equalization 55
Histogram of Orient Gradients (HOG) 236
HSV 157
Hu moment 136

I

image channels
    merging 19
    splitting 17
image color spaces
    RGB 15
image contrast
    color change, handling 56
    enhancing 55
image segmentation
    about 148
    working 151
images
    cartoonizing 67
    code, deconstructing 70, 75
    color spaces 15
    color spaces, converting 16

displaying 12
expanding 127
format, changing 15
identifying 141, 142, 144
loading 14
reading 13
rotating 24, 26
saving 12, 14
scaling 26, 28
translating 21, 24
warping 35
incidence (geometry) 32
integral images 79
interactive object tracker
    building 160, 162

K

K-means clustering
    about 146
    reference 146
kernel size
    versus blurriness 42
kernel trick 189, 234
keyboard inputs
    about 61
    interacting, with application 62
keypoints
    about 102
    aspects 99

L

live video stream
    interacting with 65, 67
low pass filter 41
low threshold value 51
Luminance (Y) 56

M

machine learning (ML)
    versus artificial neural network (ANN) 232
mage color spaces
    HSV 16
    YUV 16
Meanshift 160